BOOK
WILL SAVE
THE
PLANET

WRITTEN BY DANY SIGWALT
ILLUSTRATED BY AURÉLIA DURAND

Frances Lincoln
Children's Books

CONTENTS

Section Two

Introduction

MY CLIMATE STORY

My name is Dany. I've always been committed to racial justice. I'm also a climate activist, and I want to show how important it is that we connect these two. Our survival depends on it.

In this book, I want to walk you through not only my own story, but through those of so many others around the globe, to show how racial justice and inequality are tied to climate change and the crises we are seeing today. This is about climate justice—a way to look at how the destructive path of inequality has thrown our climate out of balance and polluted the planet. To reach climate justice, we need to understand the unjust systems that underpin most of our societies. And we need to work together to make new paths that include everyone. So let's walk together on these new paths, and I'll tell you about what started me on my own path to climate justice.

I'm from Washington, D.C. D.C. once had a thriving Black middle class, but saw a massive exodus of its upwardly mobile residents in the 1970s and 1980s. In his autobiography, Malcolm X wrote about the stark contrast between the gleaming Capitol and the government buildings—sitting beside neighborhoods full of Black people living in squalor. That was the backdrop of my childhood—I grew up in the 1990s when D.C. was known as the "murder capital," and during America's crack cocaine epidemic. Over 25 years after Malcolm X's description, I could still see this society of haves and have nots, with all the "haves" looking the same—white.

In college, I learned more deeply about **systemic** racism and **white supremacy**, studying history, **colonialism**, **feminisms**, and the **African diaspora**. I socialized with folks involved in climate activism and, while I appreciated their work, something just wasn't connecting.

In 2005, I watched the news in horror as US National Guardsmen gunned people down in New Orleans after

Hurricane Katrina, for "looting." Calling it looting seemed to depend on whether you were Black or white (two photos that made the rounds on national media showed a young Black man wading through chest-high water with food and drink supplies "looting a grocery store" while in another photo, a white couple in the same situation were said to be finding food).[1]

But it wasn't until Hurricane Sandy hit New York City in 2012 that I truly understood how climate disasters can expose society's systemic failures. As infrastructure in NYC collapsed, people who could afford a car escaped, and those with house insurance could make claims on damages. The rest of New York City was left with inaccessible public transit, damaged belongings, and homes that were no longer liveable. The majority of those with cars and house insurance were white. At that point, it became clear it was folks of color who were hurting the most in these disasters. Things began to truly connect.

I realized: climate change doesn't sit apart from inequality. Climate change is linked to inequality.

To address the climate crisis, we must address inequality. We must have climate justice. **Now let's walk together.**

BUILDING TOGETHER

I want us to join together and help build a future that makes people better off than they were before we saved the world.

COLLECTIVE ACTION

9

Chapter One

HOW AND WHY OUR CLIMATE IS CHANGING

As we start to think about our vision for a just world, we must also understand the science behind climate change.

So what is "climate"?
Let's break it down.

SUN

Sunlight travels to Earth from the Sun. Earth absorbs a lot of that sunlight, and the warmth from this is what allows life on our planet to exist. And until the last few hundred years, a big amount of sunlight was reflected back into space. This kept Earth at a relatively stable temperature, which kept our oceans, atmosphere, the polar ice caps, our seasons, and our climate in balance. It was, and continues to be, an important balance! Sadly, this is changing. Earth is now warming up, affecting our global climate and much more besides.

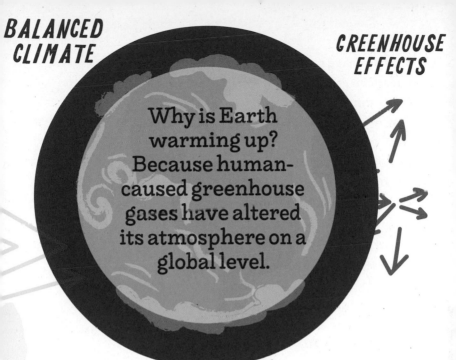

Why is Earth warming up? Because human-caused greenhouse gases have altered its atmosphere on a global level.

ATMOSPHERE

Why is this happening? Because increased greenhouse gases—carbon dioxide (CO_2), **methane**, **nitrous oxide**, **ozone**, and **chlorofluorocarbons (CFCs)**—are entering the atmosphere, changing how Earth absorbs and reflects sunlight.

Our planet now absorbs much more of the Sun's warmth because greenhouse gases are trapping it, not allowing enough of it to reflect back into space.

This process is called the enhanced greenhouse effect and it is what we are referring to when we talk about climate change and the climate crisis.

Humans have caused the enhanced greenhouse effect by burning fossil fuels and cutting down forests. Wood and fossil fuels (resources we take from the earth in the raw form of coal, natural gas, and oil) combust and burn. They create the energy we use to power our vehicles, make plastics, run factories, and light and heat our homes. They also release greenhouse gases into the air to such an extent that it is altering our climate. Not only do they cause the planet to overheat, greenhouse gases, also known as emissions, alter the chemistry of our air, water, and soil. And by destroying forests and ecosystems we are also removing one of the planet's methods of reducing these greenhouse gases (trees and plants absorb CO_2 and release oxygen). **We are putting Earth's delicate ecosystems and weather patterns out of balance.** This enhanced greenhouse effect does more than heat up the planet. It leads to rising sea levels, putting low-lying communities at risk. It increases ocean acidification that harms marine life, and it gives us more extreme weather such as flooding, hurricanes, and wildfires. Extracting fossil fuels poisons the air, water, and soil, causing habitat and wildlife loss and human suffering.

> "Global warming" isn't quite the right term—the issue is more complex than just heat.

These knock-on effects make climate change a "threat multiplier," with many outcomes yet to be fully seen or understood. This is distressing, and it is our new reality—so our next question needs to be: "**Why** are we doing this?"

Just melting ice?

Rising sea levels from melting polar ice caps show us how a "threat" can multiply, with numerous knock-on effects. For thousands of years, the Arctic and Antarctic have served as the planet's refrigerator. Because they're covered in white snow and ice, they reflect heat back into space, which balances out other parts of the world that absorb heat.

However, less ice means less reflected heat, and leads to more intense heatwaves worldwide. With these come droughts, water and food scarcity, and wildfires. It also means more extreme winters: the polar jet stream—a high-pressure wind circling the Arctic—is destabilized by this warmer air and dips south, bringing bitter cold.

Warmer temperatures thaw permafrost—the permanently frozen ground underneath the ice, to release methane. What does methane do? It further traps the Sun's heat in the atmosphere. Melting ice becomes so much more than water.

Why are we cutting down our forests and burning fossil fuels when it is so bad for the planet?

The simple answer is: to power our modern age. But there are many layers within this, mostly to do with the systems of inequality that we already touched on, and which we will delve into further. Seen through a climate-justice lens, we are harming the planet because our toxic systems place profit-making above the health of people and the planet. The term for this, **extractive capitalism** (we go into this much more on page 81), goes some way to explain why we continue to have "business as usual" despite a clear climate crisis.

Let's return to melting polar ice caps to explore how profit above planet works.

Melting ice is a bad thing, right? Not to everyone. Less ice improves access to remote wilderness that can be stripped and mined. It also offers new trade routes, used by the likes of cargo ship *Exxon Valdez*, until it ran aground in 1989, spilling 11-million gallons of oil into a pristine Alaskan wilderness nearly 20 times larger than the Gulf of Mexico.[4] That ship was towed away, and repaired to sail again, leaving the communities it polluted with long-term costs. Over 30 years later, oil lingers at Prince William Sound, and orcas and seabird populations still haven't recovered. So who, exactly, is profiting from melted ice?

We need change. Now.

ACTIVITY

Start your own climate-change diary. Have you seen climate changes in your local area? What could have caused them? There may have been more rain, but why? Think, too, about the effects on your community. Rain can lead to floods, or mud. How has your area reacted to these changes and events?

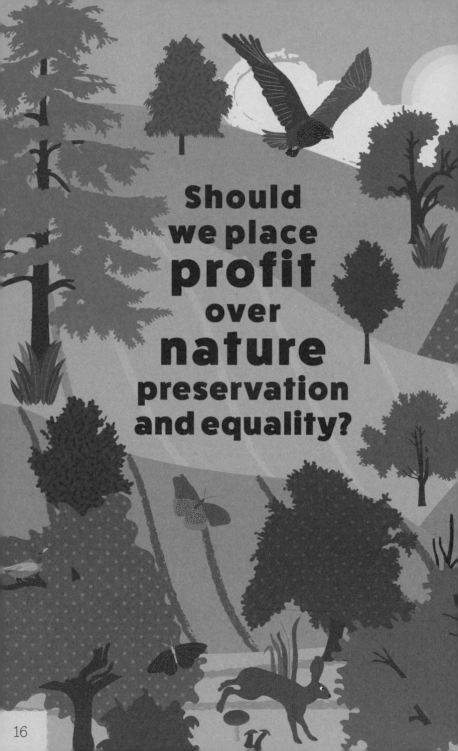

Will we choose short-term profit over long-term ecological loss and destruction?

Chapter Two
WHAT IS CLIMATE JUSTICE?

THERE
IS NO
PLANET B

The phrase **"racial justice is climate justice"** is common among climate activists these days. Often when people say this, they mean:

"I acknowledge that non-white people exist, that racism is real and, as such, Black, Indigenous, and/or People of Color (BIPOC) will suffer the most at the hands of a changing climate."

A few years ago, I published an essay about being a Black climate activist after police officer Derek Chauvin killed George Floyd and people across the globe were mobilizing for the protection of Black life at the hands of the police. In that essay, I argued that it is essential for climate activists to join the movement for racial justice. This is not only because there are deep ties between white supremacy and the climate crisis that I touch on more explicitly later in this chapter, but because whenever there's energy around a group of people or a set of communities with similar values and beliefs on social justice, we need to share our resources and deepen our solidarity to build power in the collective fight for a better future. Soon after, I got an email from a white, **cis-het**, male climate activist about how much he loved the piece, but he just wished that we could mobilize the people on "our side"—the side of racial justice— to fight for the environment. In his view, the scale and threat of the climate crisis was so much more significant than the threat of white supremacy, and People of Color, especially Black people, were most at risk from climate change anyway. I didn't reply to that email. But for you, I will break it down:

> I am a Black person in the United States. There is not a single day I don't worry about the police injuring, traumatizing, or killing someone who I love. I feel like the "school-to-prison" pipeline, which is fueled by extractive capitalism and systemic racism, could take people that I love away from me on pretty much any day.

Similarly, there are people across various communities, societies, and countries who are fighting oppressive systems that are more urgent than the climate crisis. **Immigration** crises across both Europe and the Americas are another example— whether people are fleeing because of war, drought, famine, or natural disasters such as hurricanes, a person or community's need for immediate survival has to take precedence.

WHITE

When I say that "climate justice is racial justice," I mean this:

The systems that created the climate crisis have been in place for hundreds of years. These systems — white supremacy, **heteropatriarchy**, and extractive capitalism — work in concert to directly harm people and poison the planet. We must dismantle these systems in order to rebuild a world that upholds human dignity and heals our relationships with the natural world. Climate justice is not about pushing your own agenda on people who are already suffering from the systems that enabled the climate crisis.

Climate justice is about
building power to fight against
exploitation and inequality.
It's about organizing together
to build community,
for everyone.

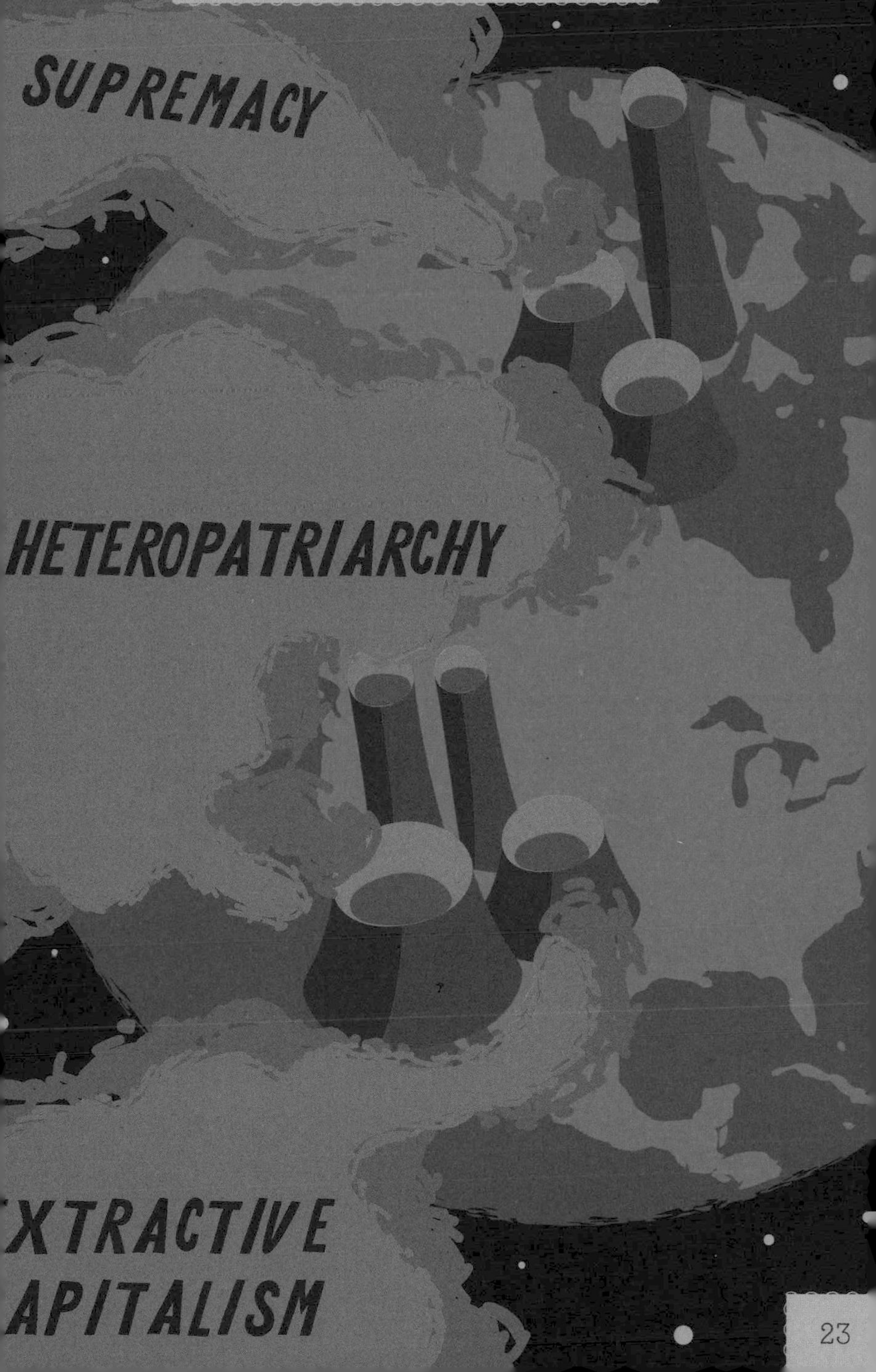

SUPREMACY

HETEROPATRIARCHY

XTRACTIVE

APITALISM

23

Humans have been extracting resources and changing our landscapes for some time, but we can thank Europeans in the 15th and 16th centuries for taking this to a whole new level. Believing humans existed separately from the natural world, and showing little concern for any ecological impacts, Europeans pillaged their land on a vast scale to make money. They then set their sights on doing the same in lands across the seas. At this time, most people on the planet were living in relative harmony with the natural world. European colonizers soon overturned this, deciding that these people weren't civilized or intelligent, which laid down the justification for centuries of further racial violence and oppression. Pushing their notions of separateness, white supremacy, and extractive capitalism across the globe, European colonizers erased important

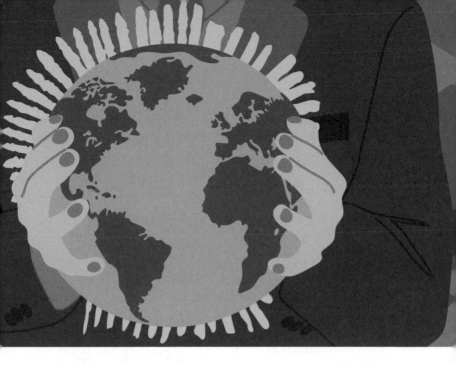

ancestral knowledge about how to care for the new environments they found themselves in. One example of this is wildfires. Indigenous people across North America would regularly start small, contained fires as a way to help tend their local forested areas. These fires would limit the amount of dry brush, preventing kindling from multiplying and ensuring that spontaneous, naturally-occurring fires were manageable. From the 19th century, European colonists in North America began to force Indigenous people from their own land and wrote laws forbidding regular small burnings in the forest. Today, we see wildfires rage across the West Coast, with Indigenous elders from the Pacific Northwest advocating a return to traditional fire lighting to control the fires.

From the 1950s to the 1970s, however, people across the planet were fighting for and winning independence from this colonialism, as well as fighting for women's rights and **civil rights** for Black, **queer**, and Indigenous people as a whole. At the same time, a new wave of environmentalism emerged as people began to feel the impacts of **industrialization** on the natural world.

Although these environmental groups overlapped with significant environmental justice campaigns (such as the Memphis Sanitation Workers Strike that Dr. Martin Luther King, Jr. was working with when he was killed in 1968), many focused on preserving nature, creating expensive wildlife reserves, and ending animal extinction. This has since proved misguided. While they saw themselves as the planet's protectors, these groups and their ideas were often simply creating more space for privileged people to enjoy nature while carrying on with the oppressive systems and white supremacy that had driven a wedge between people and nature in the first place. For example, many national parks and reserves are within areas where Indigenous people were forced from their land— disallowing Indigenous folk to use this land in traditional ways. So you have to ask: "Who is the land being saved for?"[5]

Mainstream environmental movements can also miss the bigger picture of climate justice, focusing on reducing waste, or buying an electric vehicle, for example. These play a role in climate solutions, but focusing on individual choices can often overlook the need for systemic change, and it can create a divide, for example, between those who can easily make shifts in their purchases, and those who cannot. This can lead to significant tensions between individually focused environmentalists and people working for equity, justice, access, and inclusion.

Environmental movements that don't focus on inequality and climate justice need to step up. It's time for something new.

Chapter Three

WHERE ARE GREENHOUSE GASES COMING FROM?

We know increased greenhouse gases are causing climate change, and that some of our attitudes and larger systems are helping to worsen this pollution, but let's look closer: **where** is it all coming from? Knowing this helps us to know where to stop it.

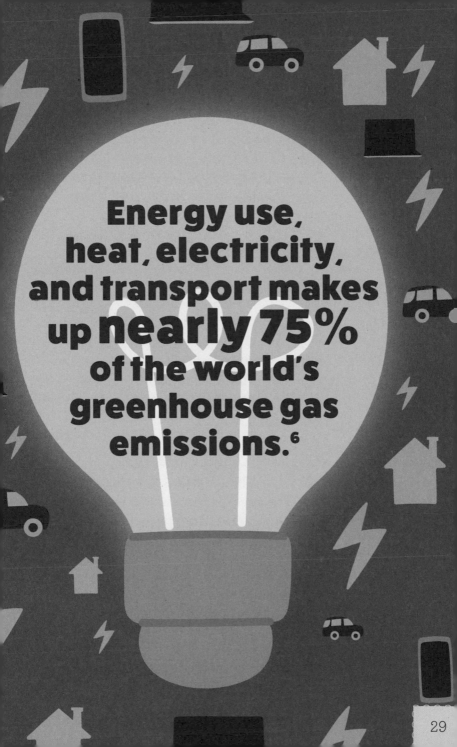

Energy use, heat, electricity, and transport makes up **nearly 75%** of the world's greenhouse gas emissions.[6]

We emit billions of tons of greenhouse gases a year into the atmosphere. **One-quarter of these emissions— about 10 billion tonnes—comes from the "stuff" we make**. This includes making iron, steel, and other metals, processing food and tobacco, turning wood into paper and pulp, and generally producing base materials that we then use to make more complex things, like your cell phone, your clothes, your windows, even the cement to make our buildings. **Right now, almost all this stuff requires us to extract and burn fossil fuels.** They create the heat and electricity to power the machinery that extracts the natural resources—metals, wood, rubber, oil, wheat, sand—for these items. The same goes for processing them and putting each component together before they are bought and used.

The energy required—
and the fossil fuels
extracted, used, and spewed
into the atmosphere—
to make, for example, one pair
of sneakers, probably makes
us want to slow down our
consumption of these items.
But this is not all of the story.
We need to shift the entire
pattern of consumption and our
extractive capitalist systems
must change. The companies
ignoring climate change to seek
profit and continue production
and consumption must be held
to account.

Where else do they come from?

Globally, we emit nearly one-fifth of the world's greenhouse gases to power our homes, offices, stores, and restaurants. This is about the same for transport. Warmth, lighting, mobility— these are necessary in our modern age. Some solutions rest in switching to renewable energy sources such as solar or wind power, or operating an electric vehicle. But this doesn't address our inequalities—for example, you may be cleaning up your own air by shifting to renewable energy, but you could also be shifting pollution to communities manufacturing those eco-friendly solar panels. Or onto the people mining for the precious metals that underpin this technology...

To address these systemic issues, we also need collective action. We can look to energy democracy, where the people most impacted by the climate crisis have the power to decide on how our energy gets produced. We can also seek out energy supply options—an energy co-op, perhaps—that would put community needs and decision-making over corporate profit.

Food, glorious food...

Creating, cultivating, and delivering food emits nearly one-quarter of the world's global greenhouse gases. This includes deforestation, which reduces the carbon store in the forests and in the forest soil, and releases more CO_2 into the atmosphere. As we have read, deforestation is putting large ecosystems such as the Amazon rain forest under threat. **Monocrops** and crop burning, as well as methane production by livestock and manure in what were once forested areas, multiply the initial threat and deepen the issue.

While changing our eating habits is not enough to create measurable change in the climate, value-driven, collective action on what we eat and how we buy and produce food will reduce emissions. And if we make mindful decisions, showing support for small, local farms, for example, we're moving our money and resources away from the old systems. This helps us build the systems and society we truly want to see.

WHO MAKES THE MOST GREENHOUSE GASES?

Let's take a look at 2020 CO_2 emissions, by regions.[7] CO_2 emissions come from burning coal, natural gas, oil, and the production of industrial waste and **non-renewable** waste. The top three CO_2-emitting regions were:

CHINA
(10.67 billion tons)

NORTH AMERICA
(5.78 billion tons)

EUROPE
(4.95 billion tons)

Together, these three regions emitted about 60% of global CO_2 emissions for 2020. In contrast, the African continent emitted less than one-quarter of North America's totals alone. The Russian Federation still emitted 250 million tons more CO_2 than all of Africa, and India produced double. **A vastly disproportionate amount of emissions are coming from the Global North**, a term describing the richest and most industrialized countries that are mostly in the Northern Hemisphere.

Emissions inequality

When these emissions are looked at per capita, or per person, within each country or region, inequalities become even more apparent. The global average level of CO_2 emissions in 2017 was 4.8 tons per person, yet countries such as the United States, Australia, and Canada each produced more than three times these amounts.

The planet's lowest per-capita CO_2 emissions are in Africa. The Democratic Republic of Congo, for example, produced 60 pounds of CO_2 emissions per person in 2020, or about 2.5 ounces of emissions per person, per day. Compare this to the US, which emitted 78 pounds of CO_2 emissions per person, per day, in that same year.

I don't know about you, but this doesn't feel like equality.

ACTIVITY

How does your community use energy? How do they light and heat their homes, office, schools, and stores? Are there community energy projects in your area? If not, what first steps need to be taken to start one?

Chapter Four

CLIMATE TIPPING POINTS

ENTRANCE

AVOIDING THE POINT ...

We're going to talk about what is to come.

Climate tipping points are events triggered by climate change that represent a "point of no return" when it comes to our ability to continue to live in the way we do on this planet.

This can sound pretty frightening. We live in a carefully balanced ecosystem and people have been messing with it for hundreds of years now, giving us very little time to change course.

It feels really big, doesn't it?

But the good news is that there's still time! While we have already reached some of these climate tipping points—and there is no doubt this is a worry—**there's still so much that we can save.**

The whole point of this book is to inform and lay out pathways for individual and collective action to build a climate-just future. By reading this, you're taking the first steps to making a positive change!

But as we enter further into the tipping points of rising temperatures, increased CO_2 levels, and ocean acidification, we enter a tense state. What we do or don't do together could change the fate of the entire system.

Think of that moment when you're moving forward and you're next in line for a busy rollercoaster. Once you get on, it will lurch painstakingly upward and drop— and there's not much you can do to stop it from happening once you're there. But right now, you can still leave that line...

Knowing about these tipping points, and the importance of these ecosystems, will help us avoid that rollercoaster "drop."

Our first tipping point is forests. About 75% of the 3,000 plants that are active against cancer cells are found in tropical rain forests. Thanks to mass deforestation, these ecosystems are losing about 137 plant, animal, and insect species DAILY— the highest rate of species extinction in the last 65 million years.[8] And then there are the foods they provide: avocados, coconuts, oranges, lemons, bananas, pineapples, mangos, corn, rice, yams, black pepper, cayenne, cloves, ginger, turmeric, coffee, vanilla, cashews...

Cutting down forests increases air and water pollution. It worsens soil erosion (the removal of the most fertile top layer of soil that helps grow crops and vegetation) and tropical malaria outbreaks, and releases CO_2 into the atmosphere, leaving us with fewer trees to provide crucial oxygen for us to breathe.

OUR AMAZON LUNGS

Producing 20% of Earth's oxygen, the Amazon represents over 50% of the world's tropical rain forests.

One of the most diverse places on Earth, it is home to 10% of the world's species, including as many as 80,000 plant species, hundreds of types of frogs, and 2.5 million species of insects. There are more types of fish there than in the entire Atlantic Ocean, and one in five of all the world's birds live in the Amazon.

The Amazon rain forest generates half of its own rainfall—but deforestation, driven by corporations growing soy and cattle for export, is wreaking havoc. In 2019, there were 74,000 fires in Brazil—wildfires and those deliberately set to clear for crops. The Amazon is losing roughly a football field of forest every minute.

About 500 years ago, there were about 10 million Indigenous people living in the Amazon—but today there may be fewer than 200,000. It is an absolute desolation of peoples.

If the Amazon reaches a point from which it cannot recover, and this is not far off, the impacts will be felt around the world.

A few more "drops"...

A temperature increase of 3 degrees Celsius:
This would forever alter coastlines across the world,
with more extreme weather events. And, of course,
as ice sheets melted, sea levels would rise. If the West
Antarctic Ice Sheet (WAIS) melted, global sea levels
would rise by nearly 11 feet. Fiji, and half of Manhattan,
would be under water.

**Mass bleaching of coral reefs, and ocean
acidification:** If too hot, coral expel the algae inside
them. Without algae, the coral—and eventually the
entire reef they have built—starve, leaving behind
sad white skeletons. The ocean is also at risk from
overfishing, pollution, and acidification (when
increased CO_2 enters the water, it changes its
chemistry). Seawater has become 30% more acidic
in the past 200 years, with marine life struggling
to adapt. If marine life were to drastically reduce,
hundreds of millions of people would lose their main
food source. As people struggled to find food,
we would begin to enter the territory of climate
collapse, which we will discuss in the next chapter.

These tipping points are a worry. But think of what we can still hold on to.

ACTIVITY

Now take a breath.
The best way we can face the realities of climate change is to refuse to give up hope in the face of worrying news.

You may want to read forward in the book to find out ways we can work to slow down or reverse the effects of climate change.

Try to list five things that give you hope for a better future world.

Read them out loud or make them into a poster, even a T-shirt, to keep you going!

By understanding the realities of climate change, we can look at whole system change.

We can focus on justice rather than quick fixes.

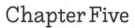

Chapter Five

AVERTING CLIMATE COLLAPSE

Don't go on that ride...

In my work, I often find myself talking about climate collapse. Climate collapse, I explain, is what we're racing against. Climate change is already here.

We're racing to make sure we're able to stop climate change in its tracks so that we don't hit the tipping points we've touched upon that will lead to ecosystem collapse.

Humans are in control of climate change. For now. We haven't had so many of the climate tipping points yet that a climate collapse is a foregone conclusion. The fossil-fuel-related greenhouse gases that humans are emitting could just...

stop.

It is in our power to collectively work toward stopping greenhouse gas emissions, extractive capitalism, inequality, and the destruction of our natural environment. With knowledge, hope, and solidarity, we can fight globally for a deep justice that allows us to heal our relationship with Earth and one another for the long run.

First, though, we must understand what's at stake, to help communicate the urgency of the moment clearly and without compromise.

The truth is that our global food and water systems are already suffering. Climate-change-related droughts and extreme weather are worsening this, reducing access to clean water and affecting food production and distribution. Water scarcity—where demand for water exceeds supply and where available water resources are approaching or have exceeded sustainable limits—causes conflict, poor health, and disease. Four billion people, or two-thirds of the world's population, already experience severe water scarcity for at least one month of the year. [9]

Hunger, too, is already a reality. The UN's 2021 Global Humanitarian Overview states that 45 million people are facing "emergency or catastrophic levels of food insecurity in IPC Phase 4 Emergency and above." This means they are highly vulnerable to facing "famine or famine-like conditions without urgent immediate life-saving action."[10] Food security is directly impacted by climate change, as changing weather patterns make planting and harvesting schedules extremely difficult.

In 2020, an estimated 30% of the global population lacked year-round access to adequate food." Poor nutrition and lower calories have lasting effects on young children's development, and erratic weather patterns and climate-change-related natural disasters increase the chance of crop failures. This leads to poor nutrition and hunger.

In the US, most of the food we are able to access is governed by large corporations that import food from around the globe if it's cheaper than growing it in the US. This affects our food security— if there are production issues halfway around the world, it is hard to access staples for your everyday diet.

With increasingly changing weather patterns and large corporate domination of the food industry, many food producers are unable to make enough money unless they farm "monocrops."

These enormous swathes of a single product, such as palm oil, are often not immediately edible or culturally relevant in the communities in which they're grown. For example, palm oil has been connected with severe deforestation in the Amazon.

Our global food systems are under stress, but there are ways to fight back. We can look closer to home, and bolster our own communities. We can seek out and join local groups—community gardens, drop-in centers, local farms— that work collectively.

Join or use cooperatives, if this is an option. Cooperatives—this could be a food store, an arts space, a housing association— distribute work, resources, and earnings equitably amongst their members. They work to engage with— and keep resources within— their local communities.

A costly game...

My friend Liz has a small farm outside of Washington, D.C., called Owl's Nest Farm. In the past, she could depend on "last frost" dates that would reliably offer guidelines about when it was safe to plant seedlings in the fields. But things have changed, and climate change is creating less reliable weather patterns. Now, each spring Liz plays a guessing game about when the last frost will be. Waiting too long to plant means a shortened growing season and less food. Planting too soon means she may lose her crops and will need to start over. Without these reliable last frost dates, Liz produces less food than she would have been able to even five years ago.

When farmers have to lower crop yields, they have to increase their food prices to cover production costs. To avoid debt, they charge more for what they do grow, and this cost is passed to the consumer.

Water, water everywhere...

I'm going to be honest with you. This keeps me up at night. We depend on water to live.

Many fossil fuel pipelines and extraction projects run through and immediately next to groundwater and waterways that feed into the world's potable, or drinkable, water. For example; fracking and tar sands pipelines threaten the Great Lakes, which straddle US and Canada, and hold 20% of the world's potable water.

Yet Big Oil—the corporations that drive fossil fuel extraction and dependance—remain focused on stockholder profits.

Refusing to invest in water delivery infrastructure also plays a huge role in water access and safety, as levels of lead and other contaminants threaten water supplies across the globe. This means that many communities must find ways to increase their own resilience. Since news broke in 2019 that the levels of lead in municipal water in Newark, New Jersey, were almost four times the legal limit, Newark Water Coalition (NWC) has distributed more than 50,000 gallons of water and more than 1,000 water filters across the city. As global water temperatures rise and pathogens grow in their waterways, this community is fighting for legislation to keep residents safe and healthy, and in the meantime is equipping people with information and distributing vital resources.

Extreme weather—hurricane rainfall, heavy rain, and storm surges—will increasingly contaminate bodies of water used for food production and drinking. These climate disasters can also damage our existing water infrastructure, such as waste-water treatment plants, with increased risks to contaminated water.

Water connects us. It reminds us that we're all a part of the same global ecosystem. It's a human right. And it's a great rallying point to get people to change their behavior and take action. Water scarcity and contamination are very real threats that we are already seeing. But the more we learn and understand, the more able we are to make things better, with a shared vision for a better future.

WATER IS SACRED

Mni Wiconi

In 2016, there was a huge protest against the Dakota Access Pipeline at Standing Rock, which was being constructed to move dirty tar sands oil from Alberta, Canada, to an enormous petrochemical processing hub in Louisiana (for more on these Louisiana hubs, see page 72). Protests along the construction route — the pipeline was being built on Indigenous **treaty lands** — drew national attention to Indigenous sovereignty issues as well as delaying the pipeline's construction.

The movement was credited to have been started by Standing Rock Sioux tribe member Tokata Iron Eyes, who, aged 12, called for collective action and mobilization. The Indigenous water protectors' declaration in Lakota: "Mni Wiconi" — or "water is life" — became a rallying cry for climate activists globally. A Mni Wiconi Tribal Water Summit now meets annually to highlight the importance of clean water for the health of Nebraskan communities as well as to highlight water's critical relationship to climate justice.

ACTIVITY

Think about your own connections to water. Where do you get water? Do you struggle to have fresh water? What's in your water supply — is there lead or other pollutants? Do you use a body of water for recreation or swimming, perhaps fishing? Is it clean or in peril? What larger community and habitat does it serve?

Food and water are essential.

We need them to live, and it is our human right to have clean and nourishing water and food. To survive, we need solutions.

When we think about climate solutions, we are talking about how we stop climate change in its tracks. This means talking about building new structures, systems, and ways of living.

Climate solutions in this context tend to fall into two categories—climate change mitigation and climate change resiliency (see pages 60–61 and page 104 for more on this).

Climate change mitigation works to reduce greenhouse gases— for example, by protesting against tar sands extraction to reduce fossil fuels, and to prevent pollution leaching into the water supply and poisoning the air. Climate change resiliency prepares communities for climate change. This could include working to improve local water infrastructure or strengthening your region's flood barriers. When we look at these through the lens of climate justice, we can use them much more effectively, as we will see in the next chapter.

We can aim for a livable future, where people are genuinely able to thrive.

Chapter Six

IDENTITY & PRIVILEGE

Key to the idea of climate justice is understanding that the way that we're going to experience climate change will depend on our social locations. Your social location depends, in part, on your geographic location (where you live), but also on a combination of factors that include your gender, race, language, ethnicity, nationality, class, age, ability, religion, and sexual orientation.

The term **"intersectionality,"** which was coined by Kimberlé Crenshaw, gives language to the way that various combinations of these identities will increase your likelihood of benefiting from advantages or facing disadvantages in your life. The right combination of privileged identities can quite literally mean the difference between making it through a climate disaster, or not.

LANGUAGE CLASS MENTAL HEALTH

AGE

RACE ABILITY PHYSICAL HEALTH

APPEARANCE

DISABILITY

FERTIL

Intersectionality is
a Black feminist framing of the
ways that our identities are multiplicative,
and not additive. That is, that the experience
of a disabled Black lesbian woman, for example, isn't
simply a summation of a list of those identities, but each
directly impacts the other to create a unique experience
in a world that was largely built to support privileged
identities rather than marginalized ones. Climate justice
is invested in collective liberation, another Black feminist
tenet tracing back to the **Combahee River Collective**
Statement in 1977. In order to achieve justice for all,
collective liberation means that we center the
people with intersectional identities in our
organizing work to avoid recreating new
systems of oppression at the top of
the social ladder.

SE

HOBBIES

GENDER
IDENTITY

NATIONALITY CULTURE

People with privilege, access to power, and the social mobility to escape climate disasters—think back to those who could escape NYC during Hurricane Sandy—are also more likely to be able to make individual choices that reduce their impact on the environment and climate crisis. These are also the people who are consuming the most fossil fuels through things like airplane flights, larger houses, higher consumption of climate-harming foods, and more. Yet those who have contributed the least to the climate crisis are the most impacted by it.[6] This inequality, especially when we look at it through a climate-justice lens, is often framed around the idea of power.

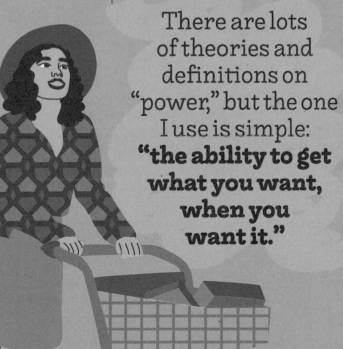

There are lots of theories and definitions on "power," but the one I use is simple: **"the ability to get what you want, when you want it."**

The Pacific Island nation of Tuvalu shows how power and inequality can have distinct effects on those bearing the brunt of climate change. Its CO_2 emissions are about 1,280 pounds per person a year, compared to Australia, which emits over 30,000 pounds per person each year.[6] Tuvalu is in climate crisis. It's expected to disappear underwater if sea levels rise. Adding to this, the expelled algae from their bleached coral reefs are poisoning the fish its residents rely on.

The residents of Tuvalu have powerful stories to tell about the impacts and risks of climate change, yet despite the enormity of the climate risks they face, they are largely ignored by those with decision-making power.

Privileged communities have more **leverage** to make their desires heard—or they might have more protections in place from the start—than marginalized communities.

They have more power. This power makes a difference to fossil-fuel companies looking to build a new pipeline.

This is why we're seeing projects in communities of people with marginalized or oppressed identities. And similarly, this is why folks on the frontlines of the climate crisis are so often living at the intersection of several marginalized groups. Because of our capitalist society that creates financial inequalities (see "Capitalism," page 78), people living at these intersections are more likely to live in poverty or financial instability.

Lack of resources makes us more vulnerable to exploitation.

Adding to this, the temporary promise of access to the wealth that building a pipeline or working for a fossil-fuel company might offer can also create conflict in communities where short-term versus long-term benefits and risks of a project have to be considered. Because of these competing interests, a key part of climate justice work is ensuring that people who are most exploited by the capitalist system have **agency** and power to make decisions about their family and their communities' wellbeing in regard to both their immediate and long-term needs. It means always looking at solutions through a climate-justice lens, and taking account of our various social locations.

Through this climate-justice lens, there are solutions to a better, fairer world. We can work to mitigate the impact of fossil fuels and keep them in the ground...

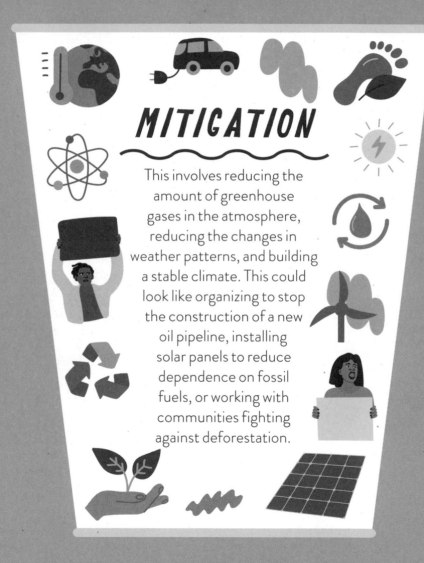

MITIGATION

This involves reducing the amount of greenhouse gases in the atmosphere, reducing the changes in weather patterns, and building a stable climate. This could look like organizing to stop the construction of a new oil pipeline, installing solar panels to reduce dependence on fossil fuels, or working with communities fighting against deforestation.

... and we can build resiliency, which is when people have the resources necessary to make decisions that protect their long-term wellbeing rather than their immediate survival.

RESILIENCY

This involves working to prepare communities and geographies to respond to climate change. This could look like building fire-resistant houses in wildfire-prone areas or learning how (or teaching others how) to grow food and invest in local food production. Our ability to adapt to climate change will depend on our relationships with people in our immediate surroundings. How can we give our communities agency and power for long-term resilience?

A really important piece of climate justice work is understanding how issues are interconnected and to then critically engage with your climate vulnerabilities and community resilience. In order to be a good neighbor and take care of those around you, it's important to understand not only the ways in which our identities intersect to create vulnerability to the climate crisis, but also to look at how we can use any privileges we have to help others.

ACTIVITY

Think about you.

- What is your social location?

- How do these intersect with each other?

- What privileges do you have?

Chapter Seven
CLIMATE STORIES

Many of us have stories about how "natural" disasters (are they natural if they have been caused by climate change?) have directly impacted our individual lives, or pushed us into adjusting our plans for the future. As an activist and organizer, I know that our stories form some of the strongest tools we have to change the world. Stories bring people together, and help us to see similarities in our experiences. They build bridges across our perceived differences. Individual people's stories help us identify systems that groups of people can then come together to improve or dismantle. Our stories and experiences sit at the heart of why and how we seek to change the world.

Here are some things for you to think about as you build your own climate story.

Where do you call home? Why?

A key element of our climate story rests in our relationship with land. And on the surface, this makes total sense, right? The most immediate risks of the climate crisis will tie in with the specific meteorological, or weather-based, events that are most likely to happen in the place where you live. Do you live on a coast where your community is experiencing increasingly violent hurricanes? Perhaps wildfires are a threat where you live, or floods? Does this year's summer feel hotter than last?

What's your relationship to the land you live on now? What kind of ecosystem are you living in? What does that look like? And what can you be doing right now to make sure that this ecosystem is set up for a long-term relationship with the humans living there?

All of us come from people who were, or still are, indigenous to land somewhere on Earth.

Indigenous people in areas such as the Amazon rain forest continue to protect the planet. They make up less than 5% of the world's population, yet protect more than 80% of the world's **biodiversity** found in these areas.[2]

What is the history of the people who lived where you do now?

What did their lives look like? I ask because I think it's important for us to try to imagine a time when people were able to live more in step with the planet. There's ancient wisdom in these communities, on how to care for ourselves by caring for our natural environment, but much of it has been lost. We can invest energy into exploring and preserving as much of that wisdom as we can, while looking to those who carry ancestral knowledge about living sustainably on this planet.

An example of this can be seen within the Coeur d'Alene tribe in the United States, which has been buying back their ancestral homelands and replanting the native grasses and vegetation that once populated it. This, along with stream restructuring, is preventing erosion to the community's waterways, helping restore the wetland habitat, and drawing in wildlife.

Who's your community?

Seek out the people living in your community today. What are their stories? Remember our social locations from the previous chapter. Be aware that people from marginalized communities— those who face **oppression** by virtue of their race, gender, sexuality, religion, **ethnicity**, class, ability, status, or other identity— stand to be even more at risk amid climate change. Think further on these climate stories, and bring these pieces to the forefront.

Take some time to think about how you identify.

This could include acknowledging your own race, your beliefs, your ethnicity, your gender, whether you are a person with disabilities, or whether you find yourself on the autistic spectrum (this is just to name some of the various identities we can hold). You may have been born in the country you currently live in, or you may have emigrated. You may have access to family wealth and property, or you (or your family) may struggle to make ends meet.

Your answers will impact how you will likely experience the climate crisis.

Depending on how you identify, or how you are seen in society by others, you will have different levels of protection against the worst impacts of the climate crisis—for example, it is no coincidence that many marginalized communities live in flood-risk zones.[3] Within our current systems, some people have more direct access to power and privilege than others, an idea detailed in "Identity & Privilege," Chapter Six.

The more marginalized identities you hold, the better equipped I believe you'll be to center community needs and promote solidarity with an eye to climate justice. Folks who are living at the intersections of these various identities need to be in the room, because they won't wilfully leave their people behind by virtue of it just not coming up. Community solidarity— and this will come up a lot— is central to all of that.

What's your goal? What's the vision you're looking to?

I grew up in, and continue to anchor myself in, strong Black communities that have borne more than their fair share of suffering since their ancestors set foot on this continent. **With or without the climate crisis, my work will always center on the pursuit of joy and liberation for all people, especially Black people.** The history of my people on this continent has been soulbreaking, but every single generation of my ancestors survived—and I owe it to them to fight for my own healing and wholeness, as well as those generations after us.

And the same is probably true for you. It might not look like the **transatlantic slave trade**, but when we think about all the violence that people have faced over the past 500 years and longer—our ancestors' struggle is our birthright. It is because of our previous generations' struggles that we are able to live much more free lives today. And regardless of who your ancestors were—oppressor or oppressed—**this struggle for freedom is what also frees us**. It allows us to shed the burden of sustaining systems that require us to lose our ability to fully see other human beings. It helps shift the focus from violence and defense to that of healing and abundance. And right now, this means fighting a climate crisis, which, incidentally, also offers us an opportunity to reorient the world so there's justice for everyone.

By rejecting oppressive systems and taking time to really think about your own climate story and that of others, we can find new ways to exist on this planet together.

Chapter Eight

CRISES UNDER THE RADAR

Massive natural disasters— fires, tsunamis, tornados—get the news coverage, and are what people tend to spend energy preparing for, but there are larger threats to our survival that are harder to see. They often happen under the radar, and more frequently to marginalized people and communities.

This is because the larger systems of inequality— racism, colonialism, extractive capitalism, to name a few—have been hard at work encouraging us l ook away. Some issues are simply not as easy to connect to climate change as a heatwave. Pollution is a good example. Some is easy to see—like plastic trash strewn across a beach. But a lot of it is harder to spot, becoming particles in the air, ground, and water, that remain hidden until they accumulate to a dangerous level or become disturbed.

Pollution might be the product of dirty energy production (think of burning coal), or it could come from factories manufacturing things as seemingly benign as clothes. We know that pollution can harm the balance of ecosystems, and it can make us sick, causing asthma, gastrointestinal diseases, cognitive impairment, and more. Air pollution also tends to be much higher in marginalized communities all over the world. In the US, there is also a strong correlation between pollution being in majority **BIPOC** communities (see box, next page). This is where our social locations greatly inform how we experience climate change. And it is where environmental racism—one of the less obvious climate threats we are facing— begins to show itself.

In an unequal society, people in marginalized communities are given less of a voice.

Environmental racism

Look at St James Parish, a predominantly Black area in Louisiana. It is part of an area known as Cancer Alley. About 50% of St James Parish is Black, and 20% of its residents live in poverty. Cancer rates in St James Parish are 50 times higher than the national average.

It's not just cancer that the people living in St James Parish are suffering from — studies have found high rates of chronic health conditions, miscarriages, and disease.

Why are the rates so high? There are 150 or so petrochemical plants that dot this region. They process crude oil and natural gas to turn into products like gasoline and diesel, and... plastics. This is polluting the air, water, and soil of nearby communities.

Now a $9.4 billion dollar 10-plant complex, belonging to Taiwanese plastics company Formosa, is trying to open in St James Parish in 2024. This plant would more than double the amounts of pollutants in the air, making it the largest producer of ethylene oxide, a known cancer-causing agent.

In response, lifelong resident and activist Sharon Lavigne mobilized her community. She spearheaded a lawsuit against the US Army Corps and the Louisiana Department of Environmental Quality for approving the plant's construction and for allowing a permit on their land. The UN Office of the High Commissioner on Human Rights called the project Environmental Racism. In 2021, the US Army suspended the permit.[12]

Disability justice

The connections between racism, capitalism, and disability shape society. Our world shows preference for able-bodied and **neurotypical** people because they are seen to be able to produce more labor for bosses to turn a profit; this is linked to the transatlantic slave trade and the labor that enslaved people were forced to produce.

Yet physical, mental, and emotional differences are natural elements of human diversity. Our bodies and brains are all different. The line between what is deemed a disability can be influenced by the ways in which a person successfully interacts with the infrastructures created with one type of ability in mind.

A building entrance without a ramp, for example, reflects a system where a person with mobility issues is simply not considered.

Last year, my coworker was diagnosed with autism. When they shared their autism diagnosis with the team, it brought to light the number of ways that our work environment, team structure, and communications were designed for **allistic**, or neurotypical, individuals. Our culture of overworking—even for a cause as urgent as climate justice—was draining for all of us, but it was proving completely unsustainable for my coworker.

When we not only center disabled activists in our work, but center our work, and how we do it, around our disabled family, we will be moving toward true disability justice. We need to re-center our infrastructures and decision making to include all the elements of human diversity.

How do climate justice and disability justice intersect?

People with disabilities are often some of the most marginalized members of a society and, as we have learned, climate change disproportionately affects the most marginalized and vulnerable folk in a community. Climate change issues highlight the areas where infrastructure and strategy are failing to meet everyone's needs. This could include, for example, not giving enough thought to how someone with limited mobility would quickly evacuate if there was a tsunami.

Some of the more mainstream environmental ideas, particularly those around individual choice, can also be harmful to people with disabilities as well as dismissive of what they can bring to discussions around climate justice. This could include condemning single-use items such as straws and cups, but ignoring the larger systems

like extractive capitalism that keep churning out "stuff." Some people with disabilities have no choice but to use single-use items—advocating the banning of plastic straws would be leaving out crucial voices on this issue.

> **Without equality, a future won't exist for any of us.**

A climate-justice approach acknowledges that those most impacted by the climate crisis should be at the front, and be the ones leading us, shown by Sharon Lavigne's campaign against the environmental racism happening in St James Parish.

With such a globe-spanning crisis, and so many fronts to face, we must focus on our collective wholeness to act against unequal systems and large corporations, and to fight against the singular focus on profit.

Chapter Nine
CAPITALISM

Why are inequalities growing?
Why is the climate crisis worsening?

You might turn and look out the window and see what is, for you, a perfectly normal day. There are no swirling signs of disasters in the air. If the climate crisis were a problem in a movie, we'd see a red sky, people running around, or some kind of big CGI disaster looming in the air.

The problem is: by the time we see that type of scenario, it will be too late to solve anything. As a result, many of us can go through our lives without thinking about the impending climate crisis. Occasionally something like a particularly disastrous hurricane, heatwave, drought, or series of wildfires might remind us about it, but for the most part many people who are not directly and immediately impacted by symptoms of the crisis can simply forget it exists.

Money.

Globally, most of us live under a capitalist system. The idea behind capitalism is that people should have many choices to decide what they buy and from whom; in this system, corporations, companies, and businesses typically try to make as much money as possible, and they're free to compete with each other to attract the most customers (and therefore make the most money). Seems almost fair. But there is something at its heart that isn't compatible with climate justice.

Capitalism tends to focus solely on one pursuit: profit.

In pursuit of this profit, corporations will often do everything possible to make people consume their products plentifully, creating a culture that has us more focused on material goods and money than on what's happening in our communities or to the planet.

For the sake of profit, many corporations promote over-consumption while ignoring the threats of climate change they are responsible for creating. To remain competitive, many businesses and companies will also offer the cheapest products as quickly as possible; that can mean exploiting natural resources, paying workers low wages, and expecting long working hours.

The terms "racial capitalism" and "extractive capitalism" are often used when we discuss climate and racial justice. These express the particular ways in which white supremacy, heteropatriarchy, **ecocide**, and other systems of oppression feed into the capitalist economic system.

Racial capitalism

is a term that describes the process of
centuries of benefit from the bodies, labor,
and homelands of Black, Indigenous, and other
People of Color (BIPOC) that has allowed European
and settler colonial governments to build wealth while
profiting from the transatlantic slave trade and the
continued marginalization of BIPOC communities.
In a capitalist system, people who have money are able
to save and grow their money through investments.
This means that typically, white families will hold
much more wealth, and it's very difficult for
BIPOC folks to be able to catch up on
hundreds of years' worth of
wealth accumulation.

Extractive capitalism is a term

that specifically addresses the
extraction of natural resources, such
as oil, from the planet, in addition to
people's labor, in a manner that is unconcerned
about sustainability or long-term consequences.
Personally, I use the term extractive capitalism
because it resonates with me as a climate activist,
but it also offers strong imagery of the theft of
people involved in the transatlantic slave
trade as well as the theft of land that
colonizers undertook globally.

Let's look again to when the many different tribes and nations of Native Americans and Indigenous Africans were generally living in harmony with nature, cultivating partnerships and stewardship of the land. Skip to the 15th century, when European settlers began to extend beyond their own ancestral lands. As they did this, they also began to extract resources such as timber, rubber, diamonds, and gold as they pleased, and on an enormous scale. European colonies were formed en masse, stealing Indigenous people's labor and land.

To justify their conquests, Europeans began to spread dangerous ideas about "man's" dominion over Earth and their superiority over other life, while also promoting new concepts of race and white supremacy. This sparked a global extractive economy that became a foundation of white supremacy. At its core,

this mindset has not changed at all and is still found in society today. It is that:

the planet exists for us to take from.

The capitalist notion that the planet can be owned, and that its resources and land can be converted into money, is driving the planet toward climate catastrophe. Colonizing settlements on Indigenous lands, extracting and displacing its people, and depleting them of their natural resources has always been a part of the extractive capitalist system that is destroying the planet.

But just because it has always been part of the system, it doesn't mean it should — or will — stay that way. We don't have to stick with this story.

Capitalist narratives

Let's look at how this colonial mindset has evolved.
It remains in the stories,
or narratives, we are told,
or which we tell ourselves.
Questioning these is crucial.

Take policing. You might think that the American police system has little to do with the climate crisis, but after the Civil War, many states in the South passed anti-foraging laws, which suppressed Indigenous and Black folks' local relationships to nature and food. It forced people to be dependent on white supremacist food systems that centered on profit. Colonizers leveraged control over nature, which has been sustaining human life for millennia, in order to wield unnatural power over people and strip the planet's resources. This narrative, that food should be farmed on a large scale and bought at a far-away store, was invented by a capitalist society, with early support from the police forces.

When we're conditioned into these capitalist narratives, we question them less. Yet the destructive path of capitalism underpins most of our climate change issues. This alone should lead us to want to shift the entire capitalist narrative, even when the connections aren't clear. For example, by prioritizing work and career over care work or artistic expression, we confirm the narrative that for something to have worth, it must make money. Monetizing labor and resources has driven unsustainable resource extraction around the globe. I try to resist this narrative — and honor labor that isn't as immediately marketable — by slowing down to do care work within the organizations that I work with and for.

Another common narrative we can fall into in the US is:

"In order to work, you need a car."

This idea allows politicians to reduce or cut government investment in public transportation infrastructure. This in turn creates a cycle where limited mass transit makes this narrative a reality. Responsibility goes from the collective, to ensure that society works for everyone, to individuals who have to work harder to meet the basic needs—in this case, a car—which a capitalist society pushes us to pay for. We drive more cars, auto manufacturers sell more cars, and we increase our fossil fuel dependence.

With everyone forced into the mindset that there is a right way or a wrong way by these capitalist narratives, we become trapped in a system that perpetuates the extraction of our labor and resources. It allows international banks to keep financing dangerous fossil fuel infrastructure across the globe, propping up corporations in their neverending quest for new ways to turn natural resources and people's labor into money. Think back to those companies that saw profit in the new shipping lanes that emerged thanks to melting sea ice in the Arctic.

Building **interdependence** and community that capitalism can't profit from—using, joining, even helping to create **worker cooperatives**, for example—is key to shifting this narrative. Climate justice is a labor issue too!

Unpicking these narratives can help us find ways to put people and the planet first.

**We can break
these cycles.
We can work
to stop banks
prioritizing
investors,
corporate
bosses, and
money over the
wellbeing of
people and
the planet.**

Chapter Ten
CORPORATIONS

Multinational fossil-fuel corporations — or "Big Oil" — are not interested or invested in averting a climate emergency; they only care about their profits, and that's what they'll protect.

To do this, they remove accountability from their actions in a wide variety of ways, including working to shunt the blame for the climate crisis onto individuals, for example, by focusing on our shopping choices, or the type of lightbulbs we use (or happily allowing other organizations or companies to promote these ideas).

Big Oil also spends a lot of money on climate denial. A 2019 study described how the fossil-fuel industry "has known about the reality of human-caused climate change for decades" and how they misled the public by funding climate denial research and campaigns.[13]

These Big Oil-funded campaigns used fake experts, promoted conspiracy theories, cherry-picked facts, and actively undermined support for climate action.

Still, many corporations in the fossil-fuel industry continue to lobby (seek to influence) elected officials, convincing them to propose and support government funding, and policies in their favor. It allows these corporations to make fossil fuel-powered energy cheaper for consumers than renewable options that aren't receiving the same subsidies. It muscles out alternative energy sources.

Many corporations also go to great lengths to have us look the other way. Through lobbyists, they seek legislation that explicitly increases the criminal charges for activists protesting fossil fuel infrastructure.

The prospect of a criminal record can stop people joining protests, which helps avoid media interest. This allows the corporation to evade public scrutiny and carry on with "business as usual." And while these situations allow countries such as the US to have relatively cheap energy, the hidden costs of climate change reach much farther. As we saw with Tuvalu, Pacific Islands and African nations are among those with the

smallest per-capita carbon emissions on the planet, but these countries are most immediately impacted by the climate crisis through flooding and droughts. [6] [7]

This is a massive injustice that cannot be ignored.

The fossil fuel industry also has a destructive habit of investing in plastics. Greenhouse gas emissions from producing plastics and microplastics (extremely small pieces of plastic that exist throughout most ecosystems) actively make

it more difficult to keep the global temperature down. Wildlife is suffering, particularly in the oceans, where plastic is entering and disrupting the food supply of birds and marine creatures. Gas emissions from plastic production alone could reach over 1.34 billion tons per year, and studies suggest that two-thirds of the plastic produced to date is still in the environment. [14] [15]

We're now locked into a plastic future that will be hard to recover from.

With science pointing at the horrific damage caused by the fossil fuel industry, what are they doing about it?

Ultimately, Big Oil and other corporations are only doing a fraction of what they need to be doing to keep the global temperature from rising, and it's not working. None of the major fossil-fuel companies have pledged to stop new extraction projects. Almost none have pledged to decline their oil and gas production by 2030.[16] All assessments of Big Oil's plans have been deemed as grossly insufficient by climate activists across the globe. The closer we get to the climate catastrophe, the more we need to bring these corporations to heel.

71% of global carbon emissions are from just 100 companies.[17]

Remember how we talked about how climate justice is intersectional?

These oil giants use their bloated profits to fund powerful police groups in the US. In 2020 it was revealed that the fossil-fuel industry, including multinational oil and gas companies, actively funded police foundations, to pay for training, weapons, equipment, and surveillance technology in cities such as Seattle, Chicago, Washington, D.C., Salt Lake City, and New Orleans.[18] These police forces uphold and enforce injustices toward those same BIPOC communities that are plagued by the environmental and health inequalities caused by corporate polluters—**these are often the same corporate polluters that, as it happens, are also funding those police**. The people who head up these companies understand that the climate crisis will create scarcity. They also know that, to preserve their wealth in the face of these growing inequalities, they must protect their property. **But who will enforce and uphold their unjust grip on wealth?** Seen through this lens, funding police enforcement makes perfect sense for Big Oil.

And for those of us seeing this situation through a climate-justice lens, recognizing these connections is key.

Stopping corporations from ruining the planet is a huge task, but if we are able to continue growing the collective voice of resistance—a voice that calls for justice, healing, and dignity for all life—we'll be able to make waves. And eventually, we'll be better off than we were before the climate crisis was a thing.

ACTIVITY

Take a notebook and a pen. Now, close your eyes. Think about one day in your life, from the moment you wake up, to the moment that you go to sleep. Open your eyes and, as you walk yourself through a day, make a list of all the different companies and industries that you use every single day.

- How many are owned by people who look like you and like other people in your community or communities?

- How many are owned by people with marginalized identities other than your own?

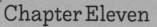

Chapter Eleven
HOUSING & MIGRATION

The poorest and most vulnerable communities, the ones least likely to contribute to climate change, are suffering the most from the climate crisis.

Climate damage is being shunted onto those who have done little to cause it, which is, simply put, an outrageous injustice. Meanwhile, those causing the climate crisis are gaining more money, and are continually rewarded. They continue to make money because people on the other side of the planet have been paying the price, and because it's been kept pretty well hidden.

Trends indicate that more and more people are being displaced due to climate-related disasters. People from the **Global South**, from countries such as Eritrea, Somalia, and Afghanistan, are taking dangerous trips across seas and deserts, risking their lives, because life in their homelands has become untenable. These waves of migration have many root causes but, as the climate crisis intensifies, with increases in climate disasters, food insecurity, and unstable economies, the connection between climate change and migration is becoming more obvious.

Globally, more than a billion people are at risk of being displaced by 2050 due to climate disasters.[19] In 2020, the US saw waves of climate refugees from Honduras, Guatemala, and El Salvador after back-to-back record-breaking hurricanes Eta and Iota hit the region, killing 200, displacing over half a million, and decimating crops, villages, and lives.[20]

In spring 2018, an **El Niño** event disrupted southern Africa's annual rainfall. Over 10 million people in this area, particularly in Zimbabwe, were already incredibly food insecure.[21] With significantly reduced rainfall, there were major shortages of drinking water, impacts on air quality, on food and nutrition, and an increase of diseases such as West Nile virus, E. coli, and salmonella. Reduced river flow increased the concentration of pollutants in water and raised the temperature of the lakes into which the cooler water would have flowed. These higher water temperatures led to reduced oxygen levels, which in turn affected the fish and aquatic life that were food sources for local people.

The drought lasted for two years, disrupting local systems that supported communities. It pushed people to leave their ancestral homelands in search of a more stable ecosystem and political system, one that would allow them to live with the infrastructure and protections needed to survive the climate crisis in the long run.

After dangerous journeys across seas and continents, these climate refugees don't even have legal protection under international refugee law.

Those who leave their countries on account of climate change or natural disasters don't qualify for protections under international law; refugee status only applies to those who face war and conflict, or who face **persecution** under grounds of race/religion/nationality/political opinion, etc.

My friend Lyrica, a brilliant organizer indigenous to Guatemala, working with a diverse group of young people in the southwestern US, says that climate justice is: **"The right and ability to go home."**

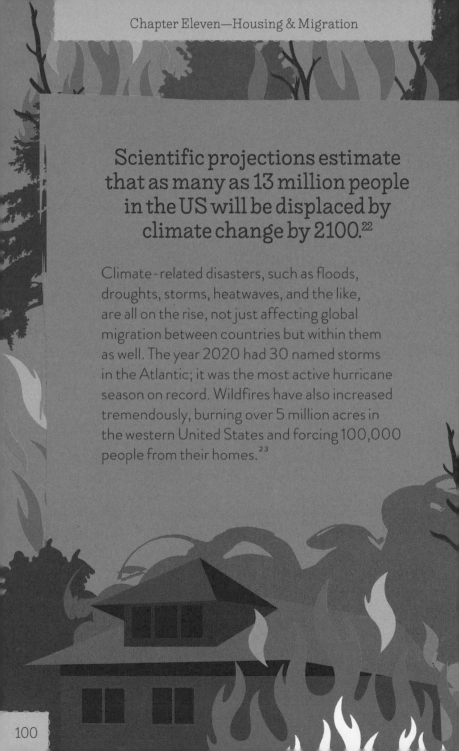

Scientific projections estimate that as many as 13 million people in the US will be displaced by climate change by 2100.[22]

Climate-related disasters, such as floods, droughts, storms, heatwaves, and the like, are all on the rise, not just affecting global migration between countries but within them as well. The year 2020 had 30 named storms in the Atlantic; it was the most active hurricane season on record. Wildfires have also increased tremendously, burning over 5 million acres in the western United States and forcing 100,000 people from their homes.[23]

People are being pushed away from their communities while fossil-fuel tycoons continue to pad their own pockets.

It's unconscionable.

But we can work together to take them down. Because this just doesn't make sense.

Households of People of Color tend to feel magnified inequalities after a disaster strikes, often making it harder for these communities to recover.

Social Problems journal ran a report on household wealth in US counties with high damage from natural disasters between 1999 and 2013. White familial wealth increased by $126,000 on average, whereas Black and Latine/Latinx households' wealth dropped by $27,000 and $29,000 respectively.[24] This gap leaves marginalized communities even more vulnerable to the impacts of climate change.

+ $126,000

- $29,000

ACTIVITY

Think about how climate refugees in your country or community navigate systems they are newly exposed to as a result of their migration.

Little Haiti

It is estimated that up to one-quarter of America's displaced people in the future will be coming from Miami-Dade County, in Florida. This brings up a whole other layer of the impacts and harms of the climate crisis—and those seeking to profit from it: **climate gentrification**. This is when land identified as being more resilient to the climate crisis becomes more valuable. Costs rise and local people can no longer afford to live there.

In Miami's Little Haiti, investors have started buying property to develop into higher-end rentals because the area sits a few more feet above sea level than other neighborhoods in its vicinity. In 2017, a real estate firm featured Little Haiti, which had almost 40% of its residents living in poverty, as one of "Florida's hottest neighborhoods." [25]

This climate-minded real estate prospecting has seen property values in Little Haiti skyrocket, with many being pushed out of the neighborhood. This forces people into more vulnerable neighborhoods. This process has also been documented to varying degrees in New Orleans and other cities across the country.

FOR SALE

CLIMATE MITIGATION & RESILIENCE:

What Can We Do?

Amid everything going on in the world, it's really hard to maintain that sense of "What can I do?"

It can feel like being an ant among titans.

But we have ways to fight! Remember, we have:

Climate change mitigation

Working to reduce greenhouse gases. This could be through technological innovation, reducing our consumption, or organizing against extractive capitalism, white supremacy, and Big Oil to stop our dependence on fossil fuels.

Climate change resiliency

Working to prepare communities and geographies to respond to climate change. It means giving our communities agency and power for long-term resilience – like helping to create and engage in a more circular economy that prevents wealth hoarding.

Let's discuss how to work toward a more just society that will heal not harm, and see equality for all.

Chapter Twelve
RESIST FOSSIL FUELS
STOP THE BLEEDING.
STOP BIG OIL.

The lion's share of carbon emissions are from the burning of fossil fuels. Step one in mitigating the damage of the climate crisis is clear: keep fossil fuels in the ground. To rebuild the economy in a way that achieves climate justice, we must stop the bleeding, not patch up the wound.

But Big Oil is addicted to oil extraction. Instead of slowing down, they employ people to work on new technologies to capture carbon. This will only sustain their extractive economic system, a system that creates extreme inequality and perpetuates dependency on fossil fuels.

Big Oil-funded scientists have also figured out how to extract oil and gas using new, much more polluting technologies. This includes fracking, officially "hydraulic fracturing," which injects a slurry of chemicals into stone and shale in order to extract deeply embedded oil and natural gas from the earth; it also includes tar sands extraction, which produces three times more greenhouse gas emissions than crude oil, and depends on intensive steam injection or intensive mining. These new extraction technologies present serious risks to our drinking water, ecosystems, and overall health.

Don't miss the forest for the trees.

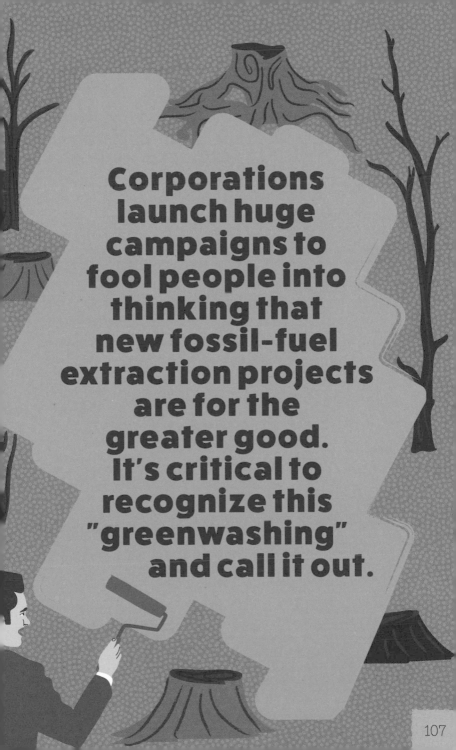

Corporations launch huge campaigns to fool people into thinking that new fossil-fuel extraction projects are for the greater good. It's critical to recognize this "greenwashing" and call it out.

We must actively pressure these companies to stop enabling the fossil-fuel industry. We need to make doing business with Big Oil unprofitable.

Yet the machine rolls on. A company called West Cumbria Mining is offering to invest $218 million in a small town on the northwest coast of the UK called Whitehaven by building a coal plant in the community.[26] This backward plan is the first newly proposed coal plant in the UK in decades—the project promises to bring jobs to a local economy that has been ravaged by its declining industries and the Covid-19 pandemic.

People need to be able to earn a livelihood, yes, but climate justice means working toward long-term solutions, rather than selling out future generations that will grow up in a polluted landscape. We must actively pressure these companies to stop expanding their harm under the guise of "helping the economy."

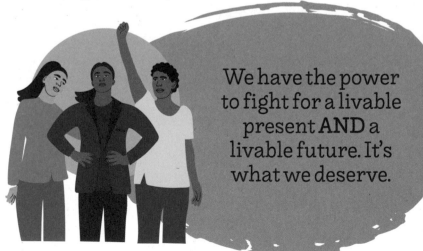

We have the power to fight for a livable present AND a livable future. It's what we deserve.

This goes beyond Big Oil itself. The fossil-fuel economy extends far beyond extraction and processing. Large international banks lend money to companies for fossil-fuel expansion projects, allowing them to expand beyond their means, and insurance companies are protecting these companies against liability in the event that someone is injured or killed as a result of "business as usual."[27]

Let's stop the fossil-fuel industry in its tracks:

NO FOSSIL-FUEL

- Contact elected officials and ask them to vote "no" to fossil-fuel enabling legislation and policies.
- Advocate for legislation to reduce fossil fuel dependence.
- Join boycotts and media campaigns by those on the front lines of fossil fuel extraction projects.
- Look into which banks are actively financing fossil-fuel projects, and stop banking with them.
- Work with your church, school, or other institutions to make sure their investments don't include Big Oil, their financiers, or insurers.
- Talk about it! Make sure people in your community understand the impact that increased toxins and greenhouse gas emissions will have on them personally.

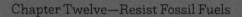

Moving industry on from fossil fuels

There can be a new way. In 2020, the Green New Deal was introduced in the US Congress, to push economic growth investments through building infrastructure and investments into renewable energy transition.

"Just Transition" is a term that people working on climate justice use to refer to supporting working people on the supply side of the extractive fossil-fuel economy in finding new careers that are not contributing to the climate crisis. That means creating jobs in the renewable energy sector for these folks. This concept also extends to economic development investments for countries in the Global South that have built fossil-fuel industries in order to build national wealth under the thumb of global capitalism.

Rather than building new coal plants, there are tremendous benefits, for example, in retraining workers in the coal industry. In November of 2015, the solar industry employed 208,859 workers in the US—more than the roughly 150,000 jobs remaining in coal.[28] The coal industry is dying, with big industries declaring bankruptcy, coal mines closing, and overall efficiency lowering. Solar energy is one way to ensure people retain employment and receive incomes while cleaning up some of our carbon footprint and breaking our reliance on fossil fuels.

This requires concentrated efforts on many fronts, between grassroots organizations all the way up to the major political spheres.

But if there's a way to heal the planet while helping people survive unemployment, doesn't that sound like a pretty good deal?

We can build new alternatives to fossil fuels, but until people with power who destroy our planet without consequence are held accountable, we'll be fighting a losing battle.

One of the most important steps in holding "them" accountable is learning who they are. This includes the people in the background who are funding policies to push fewer environmental regulations while allowing billionaires and corporations to evade taxes. These people work to push through new, damaging projects with minimal government oversight, and prevent our governments from reeling in the damage these corporations are causing.

CAP AND TRADE

CARBON CAPTURE

STORAGE TECHNOLOGY

Big Oil executives have known about the impact of fossil fuels on the climate for more than 40 years. Since then, they have funneled large amounts of money into political campaigns and governments that support their damaging practices.

We need to stay informed. Big Oil companies hire marketing agencies to help them fool the public. They promote a false idea that they are part of a green solution, while continuing to profit from killing the planet. They fund new technologies such as "carbon capture," which is the process of immediately capturing the carbon spewed from burning fossil fuels and often storing it underground. This gets government and legislation around the world on their side—prolonging the bleeding of fossil fuels and shifting the pollution somewhere else.

Yet there are things we can do to shift this dynamic. Political changes start in the streets, with protests and raising political awareness. But political change ultimately finds success in the ways that we govern. For example, we can start to run for office and elect ourselves.

Let's hold the fossil fuel industry's corporate bosses, lobbyists, and financiers accountable. Fire and call out the people who allow them to do harm. Elected officials get "fired" when they are voted out of office. Let's "re-hire" ourselves.

We can support climate champions, and work with community leaders to build

the electoral power necessary to change laws and access funding that is often denied to disenfranchised communities (where the right to vote has been denied or made difficult).

Let's start changing the face of what elected officials look like, so that there are open doors for people from all backgrounds to work in government and run for office. But don't assume that because someone is Black or Brown or a woman or **queer** that they have a similar understanding of climate justice or inequalities—always be aware of any of your own **biases**. As folks in my community say: "Our skin folk ain't always our kinfolk."

Support those who show up to do mutual aid—the ones who are always organizing and helping others. They aren't necessarily the people on the microphone at the rallies. Let's build and promote a shared vision grounded in abundance and regrowth, using all the tools at our disposal to grow solidarity.

Another world is possible, and it's being built every day. We're excited to invite you to join us.

YOUTH IS THE FUTURE

RUNNING FOR OFFICE

ACTIVITY

Imagine you are running for public office in your community, whether it's for your neighborhood, your village, your town, or a school board position. Write a speech—your own manifesto for how your community can affect change and work together.

115

Chapter Thirteen

INDIVIDUAL ACTION

Individual Responsibility + Creating a Culture Shift

GOOD FOR THE ENVIRONMENT

ECO-FRIENDLY

EASY TO RECYCLE

SAVE THE PLANET

Although there are benefits to making considered consumer choices, buying into the idea that eco-friendly products will stop climate change can be dangerous. It does two things: it makes you think it's enough to solve our crisis. And it shifts the focus.

It makes it **our** problem to sort out, rather than that of the government and the corporations and the power dynamics we are stuck in. **It expects people who are already suffering at the hands of the extractive economy to make lifestyle changes— and lets the polluters and the extractive economy carry on as usual.** For example, although some countries have banned plastic straws, some people need plastic bendy straws to drink without assistance—and we don't all have enough money or time to make eco-choices. Focusing on a straw distracts us from the true systemic problems. This is where greenwashing comes in again... It's a term we use to talk

about companies that want to convince you they are helping the environment—it could be in small ways such as putting the color green on their logos, or promoting a technology they've developed that uses way less water to produce an item without telling you that the byproducts of that dye are extremely toxic. **These half-truths and white lies are often used to sell products to folks like us who want to see a better world**, so it's important we do our research and be intentional—that is, we **choose** to make decisions and take actions about which things we buy and from whom.

Buying something because it's popular, or because it's easy doesn't mean it's the best choice for you, your budget, or the planet.

If you can, it is still wise to try and make decisions about your own consumption, lifestyle, and models for living that don't extract more than the planet has to offer. As demand for these eco-friendly alternatives increases, we are building opportunities to develop green jobs and businesses, even shifting the culture of the status quo on the production side as well.

More considered consumer choices can also include transportation—using public transport, reducing air travel, shifting to an electric vehicle—as well as looking at renewable energy for your home. Along with fighting for systemic change and community action, these choices can all help shift a culture

We have a responsibility to make sure that the decisions we make are moving toward climate justice, which demands that workers, producers, and all people involved are treated with dignity and respect.

of reliance on fossil fuels. Economics studies are beginning to show that those of us using our purchasing power can influence the decisions of these big producers. They want money. They want **our** money. And while we're currently in this extractive capitalist system, we might as well put it to work in our favor.

Individual and collective actions aren't necessarily incompatible. We can organize for systemic change, bringing other people along in the journey of fighting for the world that we deserve, while still encouraging individual behavior changes. In this way, encouraging personal behavior when there is intention and recognition that this choice isn't available to all, can only deepen and empower the climate-justice movement.

The "R"s...

Refuse

Simply refuse to have it. In such a "yes"-driven capitalist society, the power of "no" is incredible, especially for free stuff—coupons, magazines, coffee cups—that becomes instant waste. **Don't be lured into immediate gratification.** See if you still want it in a few days...

Rethink

Think about alternatives. Can you borrow or rent instead? Some areas have tool libraries. Rather than throw something away, can you repurpose it? Instead of buying new, you may have an item you could change to fit your immediate needs. Consider reducing meat and dairy—cattle and deforestation are significant factors in climate change.

Repair

Develop basic skills— repaint furniture, resole your shoes, darn clothes—to make them last longer.

Reduce

Be realistic about what you need! Take care in your decisions when you do buy something. Well-made, maintained products last longer and don't break down as quickly. Avoid fast fashion and opt for longer-lasting clothes.

Reuse

Ask yourself: "Can I find a way to reuse this?" Especially when it comes to electronics, clothing, and furniture, and the amount of waste they create.

Recycle

Recycling paper, aluminum cans, and plastic bottles, is still helpful. Recycling 10 plastic bottles can power a laptop for more than 25 hours. But clean them first. Non-recyclable or dirty items can contaminate whole batches of recyclables, which causes them to be thrown out instead.

Rot

There are many different techniques on composting now, including for those with limited outdoor space (or none), such as worm composting or pick up services and drop-off spots.

Zero waste

Part of consciously consuming goods means looking at the whole life cycle of an item and thinking: "What happens to this thing when I'm done with it?" The Zero Waste movement tries to address this by focusing on reducing consumer waste to nothing, keeping it out of incinerators and landfills.

But how does this relate to climate change? Most of the Global North's trash is full of organic matter. Organic matter, meaning anything that comes from plants or animals, all breaks down in landfills slowly, producing more toxins, and releasing greenhouse gases if they aren't decomposed properly. In landfills, where trash is piled on itself with no aeration (having air run through it), organic matter breaks down to produce methane, the most dangerous of the greenhouse gases. And that's the end of its life cycle.

Most of the zero-waste movement is focused on reducing our reliance on plastics, so recycling is a big topic in zero-waste spaces. Depending on where you live, the options for recycling will vary substantially. In the US, a lot of our plastics get shipped to China for processing.

Often, because the plastic isn't clean enough, or the right type, or because the market isn't favorable, a lot of our plastic still ends up in landfills — just in another country.

The perfectionism and competitive nature of the Zero Waste movement leaves much to be desired, and is not all that realistic or inclusive—we can't all reduce our trash for a year to a thimble—but also it neglects to focus on the supply chain. For example, the almonds in a bulk bin arrived first in plastic packaging, and there are issues around intensive almond cultivation and farming. Limiting our energy to reducing only the waste that we can see winds up causing harm to people who are dealing with the impacts of plastic pollution across the globe.

That's not to say we shouldn't consume less, recycle, and try to use less plastic. If we are mindful about how we contribute to the climate crisis via the inherited systems of extractive capitalism, heteropatriarchy, and white supremacy, we can work to break out of those cycles. In doing this, we create models for sustainable living that create visibility, and this is an important step in culture change. What are some things that can help us live in a more sustainable way?

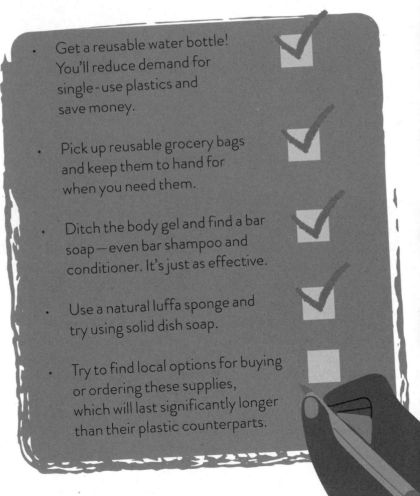

- Get a reusable water bottle! You'll reduce demand for single-use plastics and save money.

- Pick up reusable grocery bags and keep them to hand for when you need them.

- Ditch the body gel and find a bar soap—even bar shampoo and conditioner. It's just as effective.

- Use a natural luffa sponge and try using solid dish soap.

- Try to find local options for buying or ordering these supplies, which will last significantly longer than their plastic counterparts.

But please, don't stop there.

Do everything that you can to make sure that sustainable choices are available to everyone, regardless of disability, income level, geography, and so forth.

In short, **instead of wondering why people don't make better choices, ask why corporations aren't doing more to make sustainable options available.** Ask why large numbers of schools aren't teaching children about the climate crisis and the systems that have worsened it. And then see how you can work collectively to help them reach these goals.

Climate justice is about solidarity and collective action, not isolated gestures or individual egos.

ACTIVITY

Can you think of a collective action for climate justice in your community? A local co-op? A rental scheme/library/community space? Get in touch to use their services, or maybe even discuss with them ways in which you could join in and work together.

Chapter Fourteen

BUILD RESILIENCY & COMMUNITY

Remember your climate story? Let's go back to that.

How does that story look now that you've had the opportunity to think about the global impacts of the climate crisis? White supremacy, extractive capitalism, and heteropatriarchy will have us think that we're on our own in managing climate disasters, but how can we write a story that flips that script?

They'll tell us that if our homes aren't sufficiently weatherproofed, if we haven't put the time into creating an escape plan, if we don't evacuate when it's suggested, it's on us to deal with the ramifications. But it was that kind of individualistic vantage point that led us to the climate crisis to begin with. After all, **it's the pursuit of wealth for a few people while endangering the lives of billions that brought us to this crisis**.

When we can't trust the government to mobilize quickly enough and we know that corporations and the extractive capitalist

system don't have our backs, what do we do in the face of a changing climate and the related dangers and hurdles that will continue to emerge over the coming decades? First, we get informed. Misinformation around the climate crisis is everywhere. Even worse, media outlets have routinely failed to connect significant weather events to climate change and human activity. Alarmingly, major media corporations are owned by billionaires who stand to lose a lot if people shifted their attention from consumerism and popular culture to our ecosystem's health and to oppression across the planet.

The next thing we do is mobilize. We work in solidarity, together. Moving away from an individualistic mindset to a collective-centered one is one of the most powerful steps we can take to build climate resilience in our communities. Let's get prepared.

So what does community climate resilience look like?

First, get to know your neighborhood.

Work to cultivate and sustain deep relationships with people in your communities. This, in turn, helps our community asset mapping. This is when we work with our community to identify its skills, resources, material supplies, and vulnerabilities, both to support day-to-day interdependence as well as for support in the face of a severe weather event or other crisis.

I spend time talking with my next-door neighbor. I know details about her children's medical conditions that could help save their lives. I know which places on my block house folks with limited mobility, who might need help in case of severe flooding. I also know which neighbors I could ask for help if, and when, I might need it.

Being in relationships with the people who are in the closest proximity to your home and your family is one of the most important ways to build a strong foundation for climate response in your neighborhood. **If a weather event leaves a blackout in your community, your activist friends across the country aren't going to be able to help you in the same way that your next-door neighbor, who has a generator, will.**

People come up and ask me about the solar panels on my house, and I get to begin having conversations about climate justice, local environmental justice work, and my little front yard vegetable garden.

We talk about the littering in our neighborhood (there's a lot), community clean ups, and other community efforts that could make a difference in our quality of life and the ways that we are working to live in alignment with the planet.

And with these relationships, ideas, and community investment, we are beginning to build resiliency.

All this "getting to know your neighbor" business leads to something else—mutual aid and community care. Mutual aid is when we actively work with others to build networks to distribute goods and services in times of need and beyond in order to build local and community self-reliance. **It is the practice of distributing those neighborhood assets you mapped on the previous page!**

Some of the effects of climate change are slow, for example, weakening supply chains that raise the price of food that isn't produced locally. Water scarcity is another. But there are others that will be sudden, like tornadoes, flash floods, and wildfires.

For all of these, building local support networks is critical to making sure not only that you and your loved ones are able to get access to the things that you need, both now and for the long term, but also that we are building systems of support and interdependence that aren't focused on profitability, but rather on human dignity and community care.

LOCAL STORE

The human failures in our current system are often what turns these disaster moments into tragedies.

When people start scavenging to get food, water, batteries, and whatever they might need to make it through the days or weeks until a coordinated government response might be able to help them, capitalist motives pop up and call these people looters (as seen in the media coverage of the Hurricane Katrina disaster in New Orleans). Rather than focusing on protecting people and meeting their immediate needs, the US government mobilizes a police system that is often more focused on protecting capitalist interests such as stores and banks.

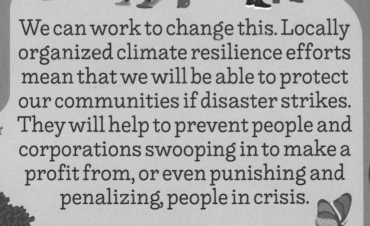

We can work to change this. Locally organized climate resilience efforts mean that we will be able to protect our communities if disaster strikes. They will help to prevent people and corporations swooping in to make a profit from, or even punishing and penalizing, people in crisis.

Covid and mutual aid

Mutual aid rapidly gained visibility during the Covid-19 pandemic in 2020. Across the globe, people organized within their communities to share resources and make sure that neighbors had access to the things they needed to get through the lockdown.

Young healthy people would check in with their more vulnerable neighbors to ask if they needed support getting groceries. Folks with cars would help others get to their essential worker-designated jobs. People would make sure that others had access to all the resources to which they were entitled. It helped our communities ride through the lockdowns, and beyond, with dignity. It helped us all feel connected to a larger community that was committed to our wellbeing.

In Washington, D.C., a complex community network was woven across individual blocks, neighborhoods, the city's eight wards, and the larger metropolitan area. It made sure that people were able to have their needs met by a community, rather than by depending solely on government systems or charities.

This work was especially important for service workers who depended on the city's dried-up tourism economy. It was taking months to be able to access unemployment funds. Individual people in these networks were able to build relationships with local businesses, organizations, government departments, and others to create opportunities to get resources to people in need.

Community members working together to meet folks' needs on the ground are always going to have a better sense of what's happening than government officials. These officials often depend on sanitized data that is focused more on policy and budgetary analysis than human relationships.

What's more, communities can respond more quickly and thoroughly to neighbors' requests than government offices and **nonprofit** organizations that are operating on a service model that checks a name off of a list and doesn't think about them again.

FREE
FOOD

ACTIVITY

What did your community or town do to help others during Covid-19 lockdowns?

Chapter Fifteen

DISASTER RESPONSE GONE WRONG

When others think they know best...

There are a lot of people with big hearts and great intentions working in nonprofit organizations, with employees on the ground trying to support people in the wake of disaster, but there are limitations to what they can do.

Coming in and making large investments without being attuned to a community's unique needs and circumstances is a form of saviorism, a pattern where privileged people — often wealthy, white folks — are viewed as "rescuing" marginalized people.
These folks might want to help because they genuinely think it's the right thing to do, or perhaps because they think it will make for good press. Regardless, allowing outsiders to swoop in to make decisions about what's best for a community is never a solution to systemic problems.

After Hurricane Katrina in 2005, celebrities and larger organizations raised millions of dollars to help rebuild the Lower Ninth Ward in New Orleans, the corner of the city hardest hit by the hurricane.

Sadly, many of these efforts were incredibly flawed from the outset, with housing designs that didn't appear to be developed with New Orleans' climate in mind. Roofs on the decks were built flat, rather than slanted. This allowed water to pool, breeding mosquitoes and growing dangerous microbes. Some houses have also had serious mold issues because construction materials were inadequate for Louisiana's damp swamp climate.[29]

What these types of projects did here was charity. Charity presumes that the people with money, who have navigated our oppressive systems adeptly and who have often inherited their privilege and wealth, know what's best for people who are oppressed by those systems.

Mutual aid, at its root, honors people's requests, which are based on their own understanding of their own situation, and works to make sure those requests are met, without questioning their motives or judgement. It flips the script of wealthy donors deciding how aid is distributed. Mutual aid puts the power into the hands of people who are most vulnerable to systemic violence, which is most acutely visible during and after crisis moments. Mutual aid is about solidarity.

Unlike charity, solidarity belongs to everyone. At its core, it understands that the people most impacted by climate changes, or disasters, or crises, know what's best for them and their communities. More importantly, solidarity inherently disrupts the systems of extractive capitalism, white supremacy, and heteropatriarchy by placing power in the hands of the impacted rather than the rich.

Please don't take this to mean that I don't think people with wealth have a role to play in mutual aid work. Moving money to mutual aid efforts is invaluable, and something anyone who is able to should do anytime there is need. Give as generously as you can. Even without the control or the media communications you might have with traditional charity contributions, you'll do much more good within a community than you might do by donating to a group of outsiders who are paying corporate bosses with your donation in addition to trying to meet on-the-ground demands.

Profiting on misery

Naomi Klein writes about a concept known as "disaster capitalism," which is a practice of taking advantage of major events (like hurricanes, heatwaves, or wildfires) to pressure people into accepting policies that would otherwise be seen as unacceptable.

> Governments and corporations will take advantage of people's fear and confusion to push forward "solutions" that create even more opportunities for corporations to extract wealth from communities that are already suffering.

What might that look like? In February 2011 there was a large winter storm in Texas, which rarely sees sub-zero temperatures. The demand for energy to warm people's homes surged, outpacing the capacity of the grid, and there were deadly blackouts across the state. One hundred and eleven people died as a result.

To make matters worse, because US energy companies base their cost on demand, some Texan's bills soared to more than $15,000 for one month (more than a year's wages if you worked a full-time minimum wage job).[30] People's needs for life-saving energy were treated in a similar way that a department store might raise the price of a sought-after Christmas toy. Government programs eventually offered support for those with exorbitant bills but that didn't change the fact that energy companies and banks invested in fossil fuels made hundreds of millions of dollars in profits from Texans in a crisis.

> **Taxpayer dollars subsidized corporate profits in a way that would never have been acceptable if the scenario hadn't been triggered by a crisis.**

That's how disaster capitalism works. It seeks to profit from demand, regardless of whether it is a humanitarian disaster or a plastic toy. And if we're not careful, something similar could happen with every single hurricane, drought, pipeline leak, fire, and flood in our future.

GOVERNMENT SUPPORT

TAXES

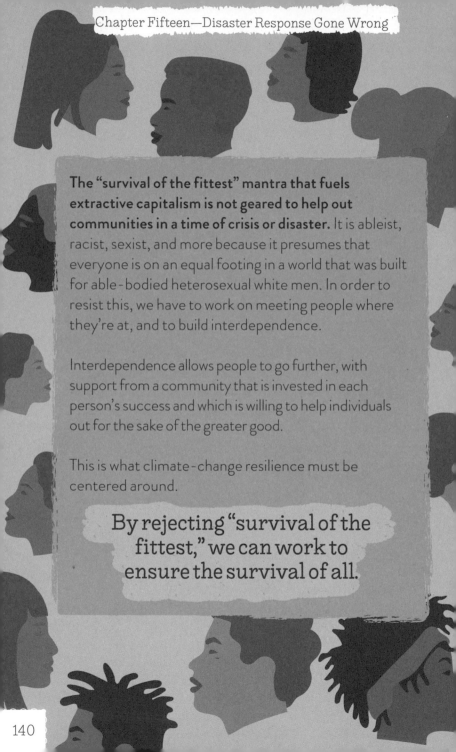

The **"survival of the fittest" mantra that fuels extractive capitalism is not geared to help out communities in a time of crisis or disaster.** It is ableist, racist, sexist, and more because it presumes that everyone is on an equal footing in a world that was built for able-bodied heterosexual white men. In order to resist this, we have to work on meeting people where they're at, and to build interdependence.

Interdependence allows people to go further, with support from a community that is invested in each person's success and which is willing to help individuals out for the sake of the greater good.

This is what climate-change resilience must be centered around.

By rejecting "survival of the fittest," we can work to ensure the survival of all.

ACTIVITY

Look to cultivate and sustain deep relationships with people in your communities. Think about how the following could work in your neighborhood:

- **Community asset mapping**—work with people in your community to identify the skills, resources, and material supplies that people can share, both to support day-to-day interdependence as well as to support one another in the face of a severe weather event or other crisis.

- **Mutual aid**—actively work with others to build networks to distribute goods and services in times of need—and beyond—in order to build local and community self-reliance.

- **Emergency planning**—work with your family and those who live close to you to make a plan to stay safe in the case of a severe weather event or other emergency.

- **Community organizing**—bring people in your community together to build new systems. Advocate with local government to implement climate mitigation and resilience policies to make sure that people are prioritized in the face of the changing climate landscape.

Chapter Sixteen

BUILDING NEW

Here's a big fact: the wealth gap is 25% larger between the world's richest and poorest countries than it would be without the climate crisis.

A 2019 study found that temperature changes have helped cooler countries in the Global North, while harming economic growth in countries in the Global South[31]. Chances are, if you're in the United States or the United Kingdom, your country has benefited from the climate crisis economically. We need big changes. For centuries, people have been exploited and harmed in the name of our toxic systems, which go directly against the best interests of the majority of life on this planet, including most humans.

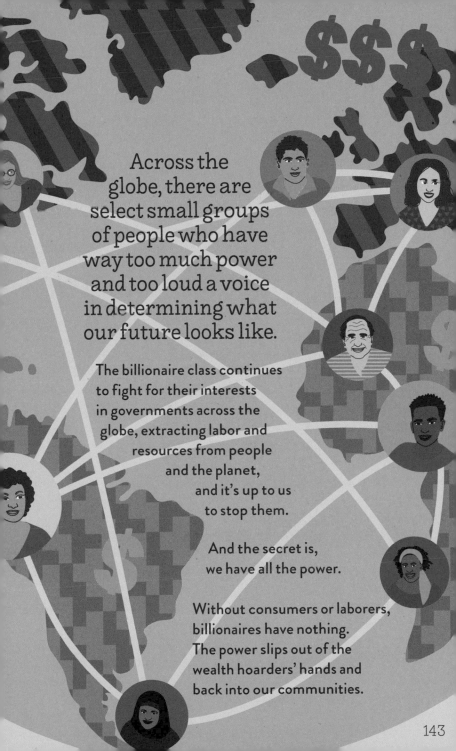

Across the globe, there are select small groups of people who have way too much power and too loud a voice in determining what our future looks like.

The billionaire class continues to fight for their interests in governments across the globe, extracting labor and resources from people and the planet, and it's up to us to stop them.

And the secret is, we have all the power.

Without consumers or laborers, billionaires have nothing. The power slips out of the wealth hoarders' hands and back into our communities.

How do we stop the destruction?

We focus on healing, growing, and building a new economy.

We've lived our whole lives being taught that we need to focus on taking care of ourselves and that our future success depends on hard work and the individual decisions we make. Go to school. Save money. Work hard. Get rich (or at least, comfortable).

But we know that systems of oppression all impact our ability to play that game.

This is why mutual aid and solidarity are so important. Those people who are most impacted by the climate crisis, by extractive capitalism, and by systems of oppression, are the ones who should have the most power when it comes to building a new world, because they're the ones least likely to leave people behind. We need to follow their lead.

People aren't disposable.

And we can't allow our political systems to treat them like they are.

It is time to build anew.

Don't feed the beast!

As we've discovered, massive international banks make loans (using our cash!) to oil companies to finance dangerous fossil fuel infrastructure across the globe.

But there are other ways to bank. Public banks, which can be run by city, state, or government, offer a great alternative. A public bank isn't beholden to investors, but to the area which they serve. So instead of investing in fossil fuels, a public bank might invest in affordable housing developments, run small business creation, or renewable energy workforce training.

State and nonprofit banks such as **credit unions** can also offer a good alternative while we build a just economic system that keeps wealth in our communities and honors people and the planet.

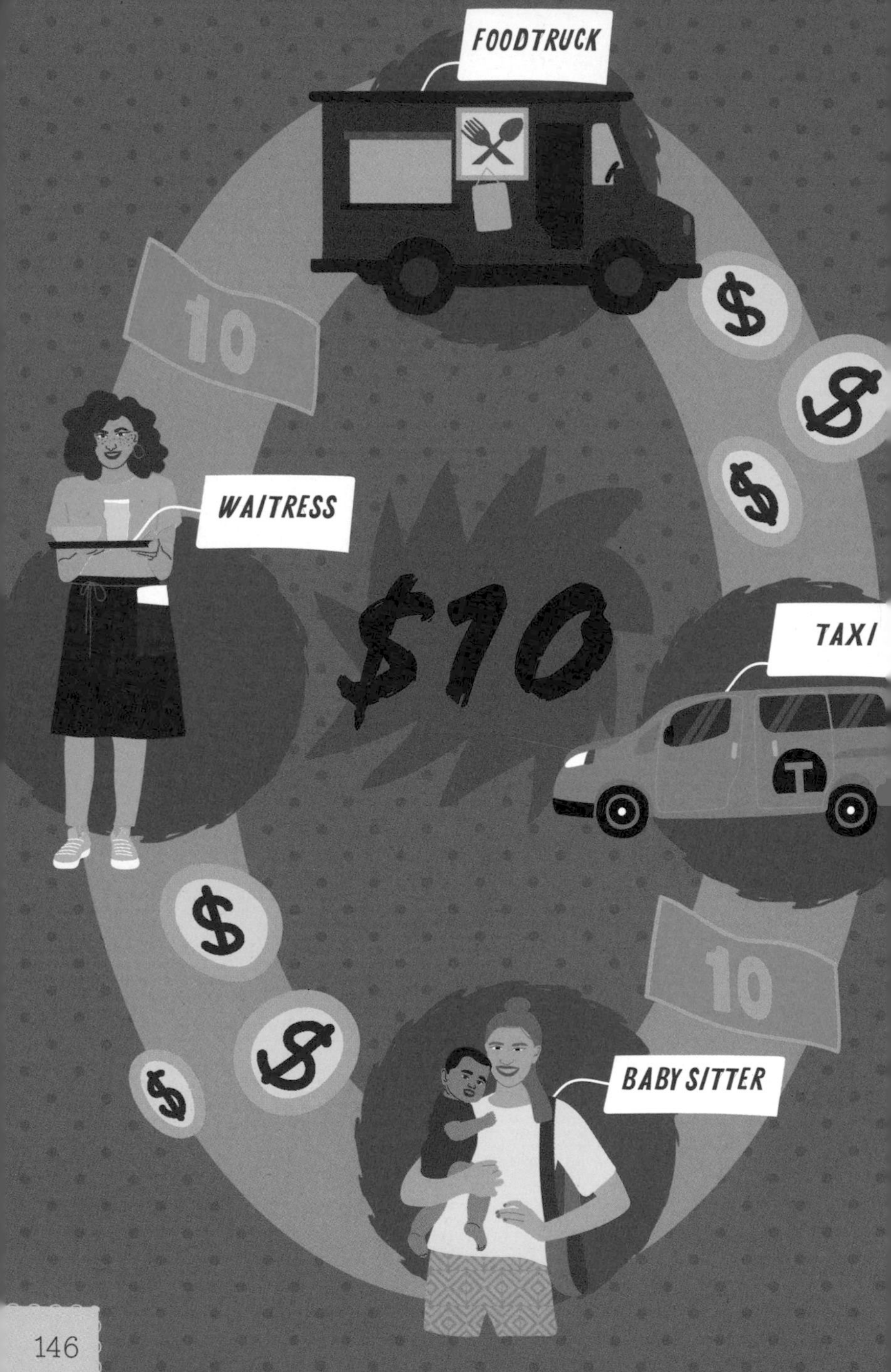
FOODTRUCK
10
WAITRESS
$10
TAXI
10
BABY SITTER

Extractive capitalism profits from a linear economy, creating waste, pollution, and a neverending demand on finite natural resources.

In a linear economy, wealth moves from Earth's natural resources directly to an owning class of people who extract the wealth from people and the planet. Also called "take-make-dispose," this economic model unsustainably throws away all it produces. It also encourages wealth hoarding, which is inherently bad for the economy. When a billionaire makes $10 million dollars, they hoard it. Its value stops there and isn't shared through the economy—it just sits in a bank account or the stock market, making more money for the wealth hoarder.

In a more circular economy, when a server at a restaurant earns a $10 tip, they might buy lunch from a food truck that is owner-run. That food truck worker might use that $10 to take a cab home, and that cab driver might pay her babysitter with that money. That $10 tip cycles three times through the economy, tripling its value.

Within a year, that first $10 could easily change hands hundreds of times, bringing hundreds of thousands of dollars into the economy. When people hoard wealth, this doesn't happen, and most people are poorer as a result.

And as you know, poverty makes it really hard to prepare for and withstand climate emergencies.

This example shines...

In the Basque region of Spain, there's a federation of worker cooperatives known as Mondragon that can help us imagine this new world—it is completely owned by its workers.[32]

The workers are in control, participate in democratic decision-making processes, and share the company's profits, rather than those profits going to the company owner or shareholders. In 2019, Mondragon had over 80,000 employees at the 257 companies that made up the federation. At each of these companies, the workers determine what the maximum pay for senior employees should be, compared to the lowest-paid employees.

Mondragon is the largest cooperative in the world. Imagine how we can bring these shared ownership and democratic workplace models into our own communities. Imagine how those could support our ability to build climate change resilience within the wider world.

There are plenty of other cooperatives in our communities already. Grocery cooperatives, for example, have been staples for decades now. Some are worker-owned and others are owned by customers (people who live in the community the business serves). Regardless of the ownership, what we're looking at in both cases is community control of business and the economy, rather than outside influence and profit-driven objectives being put above community needs and long-term impacts.

People across the globe are building a solidarity economy that reimagines how people relate to our environment to produce goods and services for everyone's needs.

That could look like small-scale farmers partnering in cooperation to produce, market, and distribute their foods to avoid corporate distributors.

Or perhaps it's advocating for your local government to invest in long-term affordable cooperative housing so that people are able to live in safe and adequate homes.

It can also look like people coming together to take control over their energy production by forming a community solar farm that produces local clean-energy job opportunities and is democratically run by the community.

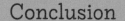

Conclusion

WHAT WILL SAVE THE PLANET?

- Circulating money through a community, rather than hoarding profit.

- Putting workers at the heart of decision-making and profit sharing.

- Creating production models that depend on recycling and reusing goods.

- Using natural resources at a pace that doesn't overtake what the planet is able to produce.

Let's build a new world to meet people's basic human needs.

We are talking about equality.
Justice for all, not riches for the few.

If we look around, and bring everyone to the table, we might find we already have all the answers.

ACTIVITY

Imagine the world you want to see.
Now write down five things you can start
to do to help make this happen...

Before you go...

Pause for a moment.
Let your body feel the grass.
Look close at what's around you,
watch a bird flying free.

Feel the chill wind,
a gust of warm air, or enjoy
the stillness.

Listen to the world:
a chirp, a buzz, a mew.
Feel the sun on your cheeks,
its rays giving life.

Think how each living thing,
each bit of earth and sky
is part of our world,
and is part of us.

Each flap of a butterfly's wings...
each time you join in with this world...
there are ripples.

Now think of the world you want to see . . .

- What will our communities look
  like in a just world?

- How do you envision we will get there?

- Who are the folks to bring on this journey,
  to keep you anchored, and give hope?

Further Reading

A Bigger Picture: My Fight to Bring a New African Voice to the Climate Crisis,
by Vanessa Nakate.

All We Can Save: Truth, Courage, and Solutions for the Climate Crisis,
Edited by Ayana Elizabeth Johnson and Katharine K Wilkinson.

Care Work: Dreaming Disability Justice, by leah lakshmi piepzna-samarasinha.

Emergent Strategy: Shaping Change, Changing Worlds,
by Adrienne Maree Brown.

Inflamed: Deep Medicine and the Anatomy of Injustice,
by Rupa Marya and Rajeev Charles Patel.

Overheated: How Capitalism Broke the Planet — and How We Fight Back,
by Kate Aronoff.

Parable of the Sower, by Octavia E. Butler.

Rules for Radicals: A Pragmatic Primer for Realistic Radicals,
by Saul Alinksy.

The Red Deal: Indigenous Action to Save Our Earth, by The Red Nation.

The Rise of the American Conservation Movement: Power, Privilege,
and Environmental Protection, by Dorceta E. Taylor.

The Story of Stuff: How Our Obsession with Stuff is Trashing the Planet,
Our Communities, and Our Health — and a Vision for Change,
by Annie Leonard.

This Changes Everything: Capitalism vs. The Climate, by Naomi Klein.

Film
The Story of Plastic, Pale Blue Dot Media, directed by Deia Schlosberg.

Glossary

African diaspora—the many communities of people of African descent throughout the world, the majority dispersed as a result of the largest forced migration in history—the transatlantic slave trades.

Agency—your power to make effective change. It's your ability to make choices and decisions.

Allistic—a non-autistic person, or someone not affected by autism.

Bias—your personal preference for, or against, an individual or group. It can interfere with your judgment.

Biodiversity—the massive variety of life on Earth, including all living things, from bacteria to mammals to the larger ecosystems they live and interact within.

BIPOC—Black, Indigenous, People of Color.

Chlorofluorocarbons (CFCs)—chemical, gaseous compounds that release chlorine when they break down, and which are responsible for the destruction of Earth's ozone layer. Found in aerosols and refrigeration. One of the greenhouses gases.

Cis-het—a heterosexual (a person who is attracted to people of the opposite sex) whose personal identity and gender expression corresponds with their sex assigned at birth. Cisgender (cis) is a person whose gender identity corresponds with that person's sex assigned at birth.

Civil rights—equal rights for all, regardless of race, gender, sexual orientation, politics, religion, social class, or ethnicity.

Climate gentrification—a process where, because an area is seen to be more resilient to the adverse effects of climate change, its value grows. Wealthier individuals and businesses move to the area, pushing out those who can no longer afford to live there due to increased housing costs.

Colonialism—the system of colonization, when a population transfers to a new territory and takes control over another group of people, often using violence and manipulation to gain and maintain power and control over land and resources.

Combahee River Collective—a Black feminist lesbian organization that gathered between 1974 and 1980 to address their needs as a community, to write about their identities and to declare that collective, nonhierarchical power creates a pathway for culture and society to defy and stamp out gender, sexual, racial, and class-based domination and oppression.

Credit union—a not-for-profit, member-owned financial cooperative.

Ecocide—deliberate or negligent destruction of the natural environment.

El Niño—an unpredictable climate pattern where the surface waters in the eastern tropical Pacific Ocean warm up, and trade winds weaken, affecting ocean temperatures and the speed and strength of ocean currents. It has often been used to describe irregular and intense changes in the weather and climate.

Ethnicity—your cultural heritage: languages, traditions, ancestral history. It is not the same as your race.

Extractive capitalism—a term that specifically addresses the extraction of natural resources, such as oil, from the planet, in addition to labor, without concern about sustainability or long-term consequences.

Feminisms—a set of social and political movements aiming for all genders to have equal rights and opportunities.

Global North—the richest and most industrialized countries, most of which are in the northern part of the world.

Global South—the poorest and least-industrialized countries, which were former European colonies and which are mostly in the southern part of the world.

Heteropatriarchy—a political and social system in which cisgender and heterosexual males have dominance over people with other genders and sexual orientations.

Immigration—the international movement of people to a country in which they were not born in and in which they do not have citizenship, but to which they want to settle in for an extended period of time, often permanently.

Indigenous people—UN definition: Indigenous peoples are inheritors and practitioners of unique cultures and ways of relating to people and the environment. They have retained social, cultural, economic, and political characteristics that are distinct from those of the dominant societies in which they live.

Industrialization—within the context of the book, this refers to the specific period of social and economic change known as the Industrial Revolution, when Great Britain, continental Europe, and the United States transformed to new manufacturing processes on a massive scale, one that was dominated by machines and intense economic growth as well as a reliance on fossil fuels and extractive capitalism.

Interdependence—a state in which two or more people, situations, variables, or other entities have a relationship that is mutually dependent on the others, and where they rely on one another.

Leverage—using something to maximum advantage.

Methane—the primary component of natural gas, also released into the atmosphere from landfills, agriculture, animal emissions, and coal mining, to name a few. It is a potent greenhouse gas that is 25 times as potent as carbon dioxide at trapping heat in the atmosphere.

Neurotypical—people with typical development and intellectual ability.

Nitrous oxide—also known as "laughing gas," as a greenhouse gas it is 300 times more powerful than carbon dioxide; it absorbs radiation and traps heat, and depletes Earth's ozone layer.

Nonprofit—purposely making little or no profit, for the greater good of society.

Non-renewable—something that cannot be replaced, replenished, or resupplied. It exists in finite quantity.

Oppression — the <u>systemic</u> and <u>systematic</u> suppression of a group, or groups, by another group in power.

Ozone — technically, this is a greenhouse gas, but it can be helpful or harmful, depending on where it is found in Earth's atmosphere. Earth's ozone layer protects the planet from excessive UV radiation, but at lower atmospheric levels, it is harmful to human health.

Queer — an adjective used by some people whose sexual orientation is not exclusively heterosexual.

Persecution — being abused, treated badly or with hostility, especially because of sexual orientation, race, or due to political or religious beliefs.

Refugee — a person forced to leave their country to escape <u>persecution</u>, food and/or water scarcity, pollution, extreme poverty or famine, natural disaster, or war.

Systematic — something methodical and planned.

Systemic — something that happens throughout a whole system (and institution) over the course of time.

Transatlantic slave trade — a segment of the global slave trade that occurred between 1500 and 1900, which saw Europeans enslave and transport Black men, women, and children from throughout West Central Africa and Central Africa, across the Atlantic Ocean, to work as slaves for white people in Europe, the Americas, and the Caribbean. It was the largest long-distance forced movement of people in recorded history, involving between 10 to 13 million enslaved Africans. Its repercussions are still being felt today in systems rooted in <u>white supremacy</u>, <u>colonialism</u>, and injustice.

Treaty lands — in the late 1700 and 1800s, the United States signed over 360 treaties (legally-binding agreements to establish borders and rules between two nations) with individual sovereign <u>Indigenous</u> nations throughout the North American continent, which ceded millions of acres of Indigenous land to the United States government. Many of these treaties have since been broken.

White supremacy — a political, economic, and cultural system in which white people control power and material resources. It is often connected to notions of white superiority and nonwhite subordination.

Worker cooperative — an entity that is owned and controlled by its members, which operates for their benefit.

Notes on Text

1. *The New York Times*. Tania Ralli. "Who's a looter? In storm's aftermath, pictures kick up a different kind of tempest." September, 2005; Social Science Research Council. Items. Sarah Kaufman. "The criminalization of New Orleanians in Katrina." June 11, 2006.

2. *National Geographic*. Gleb Raygorodetsky. "Indigenous peoples defend Earth's biodiversity — but they're in danger." November 16, 2018.

3. The Environment Agency report. "Social deprivation and the likelihood of flooding." January, 2021; The Guardian. Rhi Storer. "New homes in poorer areas of England and Wales face undue flood risk." April 27, 2021.

4. Ocean Conservancy. "Exxon Valdez: 29 years later." A Hartsig, C Robbins. March 22, 2018.

5. *The Conversation*. Prakash Kashwan, "American environmentalism's racist roots have shaped global thinking about conservation." September 2, 2020.

6. Our World in Data. Hannah Ritchie, Max Roser. "Sector by sector: where do global greenhouse gas emissions come from?" September 18, 2020; Climate Watch. "Historical GHG emissions."

7. International Energy Agency (IEA). "World energy outlook 2018."

8. Rain-Tree Publishers. "Rainforest facts: the disappearing rainforests." [https://rain-tree.com/facts.html]; Square One Publishers. *The Healing Power of Rainforest Herbs*. Leslie Taylor. 2004.

9. *Science Advances*, Vol. 2, Issue 2. Mesfin M Mekonnen, Arjeny Y Hoekstra. "Four billion people facing severe water scarcity." February 12, 2016.

10. United Nations Global Humanitarian Overview 2022. [https://gho.unocha.org/]

11. UN Food and Agricultural Development (UN FAO), UNICEF, World Health Organization (WHO), World Food Programme (WFP), International Fund for Agricultural Development (IFAD). "The state of food security and nutrition in the world 2020." July 12, 2021.

12. *The Guardian*. Cancer Town series; The Guardian. Nina Lakhani. "Cancer Alley campaigner wins Goldman Prize for Environmental Defenders." June 15, 2021.

13. George Mason University Center for Climate Change Communication. John Cook, Geoffrey Supran, Stephan Lewandowsky, Naomi Oreskes, Ed Maibach. "America misled: how the fossil fuel industry deliberately misled Americans about climate change." October 21, 2019.

14. Columbia Climate School; *State of the Planet*. Renee Cho. "More plastic is on the way: what it means for climate change." February 20, 2020.

15. *Science Advances*, Vol. 3, No. 7. Roland Geyer, Jenna R Jambeck, Kara Lavender Law. "Production, use, and fate of all plastics ever made." July 19, 2017.

16. *Oil Change International*. Collin Rees. "The fossil fuelled five: comparing rhetoric with reality on fossil fuels and climate change." November 12, 2021.

17. *The Guardian*. Tess Riley. "Just 100 companies responsible for 71% of global emissions, study says." July 18, 2017.

18. *The Guardian*. Nina Lakhani. "Revealed: oil giants help fund powerful police groups in top US cities." July, 2020.

19. *The Guardian*. Jon Henley. "Climate crisis could displace 1.2bn people by 2050, report warns." September, 2020.

20. UN Office for the Coordination of Humanitarian Affairs. Relief Web. "Central America: 2020 Hurricane Season Situation Report No. 3." November 17, 2020.

21. *Nature Communications*. Alexandra K Heaney, Jeffrey Shaman, Kathleen A Alexander. "El Niño -Southern oscillation and under-5 diarrhea in Botswana." December 20, 2019; UN. "Southern Africa; 12 million people are food insecure." November 13, 2019.

22. *PLOS ONE*. Caleb Robinson, Bistra Dilkina. "Modeling migration patterns in the USA under sea level rise." January 22, 2020.

23. *The New York Times*. Eric Thayer."More than five million acres have burned in West Coast's wildfires." September 17, 2020.

24. *Social Problems*, Vol 66, Issue 3. Junia Howell, James R Elliott. "Damage Done: The longitudinal impacts of natural hazards on wealth inequality in the United States." August 2019.

25. University of Michigan, School of Public Health. Elizabeth Santiago. "Weathering the storm: climate gentrification in Miami's Little Haiti." February 10, 2020.

26. *The New York Times*. Stanley Reed. "A new coal mine in England is stirring hopes and fears." August 26, 2021.

27. *The Guardian*. Damian Carrington. "Big banks' trillion-dollar finance for fossil fuels 'shocking', says report." March 24, 2021.

28. IREC. "National Solar Jobs Census 2020."; *Harvard Business Review*. Joshua M Pearce. "What if all US coal workers were retrained to work in solar?" August 8, 2016.

29. *The Guardian*. David Uberti. "10 years after the storm: has New Orleans learned the lessons of Hurricane Katrina?" July 27, 2015; Bloomberg Businessweek. Rob Walker. "When Brad Pitt tried to save the Lower Ninth Ward." February 15, 2019.

30. *NBC News*. Leticia Miranda. "Who's really left holding the bag for those sky-high electricity bills in Texas?" February 24, 2021.

31. Stanford University. *Earth Matters*. Josie Garthwaite. "Climate change has worsened global economic inequality." April 22, 2019.

32. Mondragon website: www.mondragon-corporation.com/en/about-us/.

Inspiring | Educating | Creating | Entertaining

Brimming with creative inspiration, how-to projects, and useful information to enrich your everyday life, Quarto is a favourite destination for those pursuing their interests and passions. Visit our site and dig deeper with our books into your area of interest: Quarto Creates, Quarto Cooks, Quarto Homes, Quarto Lives, Quarto Drives, Quarto Explores, Quarto Gifts, or Quarto Kids.

First Published in 2022 by Frances Lincoln Children's Books, an imprint of The Quarto Group.
400 First Avenue North, Suite 400, Minneapolis, MN 55401, USA.
T (612) 344-8100 F (612) 344-8692 **www.Quarto.com**

A catalogue record for this book is available from the British Library.

ISBN 978-0-7112-6889-0

The illustrations were created digitally.
Set in FatFrank and LiebeRuth
Published by Peter Marley
Designed by Vanessa Lovegrove and Karissa Santos
Commissioned by Lucy Menzies
Edited by Robin Pridy
Production by Dawn Cameron

Manufactured in Vicenza, Italy LE042022

9 8 7 6 5 4 3 2 1

MIX
Paper from
responsible sources
FSC® C101537